Your

New York

WILLS, TRUSTS, & ESTATES
EXPLAINED SIMPLY:

Important Information You Need to Know for New York Residents

By Linda C. Ashar, attorney at law

YOUR NEW YORK WILLS, TRUSTS, & ESTATES EXPLAINED SIMPLY:
IMPORTANT INFORMATION YOU NEED TO KNOW FOR NEW YORK RESIDENTS

Copyright © 2011 Atlantic Publishing Group, Inc.
1405 SW 6th Avenue • Ocala, Florida 34471 • Phone 800-814-1132 • Fax 352-622-1875
Web site: www.atlantic-pub.com • E-mail: sales@atlantic-pub.com
SAN Number: 268-1250

Library of Congress Cataloging-in-Publication Data

Ashar, Linda C., 1947-:
  Your New York wills, trusts, & estates explained simply : important information you need to
know for New York residents / by Linda C. Ashar.
     p. cm.
  Includes bibliographical references and index.
  ISBN-13: 978-1-60138-412-6 (alk. paper)
  ISBN-10: 1-60138-412-2 (alk. paper)
  1. Estate planning--New York (State) I. Title.
  KFN5195.A836 2010
  346.74705'2--dc22

                        2010016810

Printed in the United States

PEER REVIEWER: Marilee Griffin • mgriffin@atlantic-pub.com
PROJECT MANAGER: Melissa Peterson
ASSISTANT EDITOR: Katy Doll • INTERIOR DESIGN: Rhana Gittens
FRONT & BACK COVER DESIGN: Jackie Miller • millerjackiej@gmail.com

Printed on Recycled Paper

We recently lost our beloved pet "Bear," who was not only our best and dearest friend but also the "Vice President of Sunshine" here at Atlantic Publishing. He did not receive a salary but worked tirelessly 24 hours a day to please his parents. Bear was a rescue dog that turned around and showered myself, my wife, Sherri, his grand-

parents Jean, Bob, and Nancy, and every person and animal he met (maybe not rabbits) with friendship and love. He made a lot of people smile every day.

We wanted you to know that a portion of the profits of this book will be donated to The Humane Society of the United States. *–Douglas & Sherri Brown*

The human-animal bond is as old as human history. We cherish our animal companions for their unconditional affection and acceptance. We feel a thrill when we glimpse wild creatures in their natural habitat or in our own backyard.

Unfortunately, the human-animal bond has at times been weakened. Humans have exploited some animal species to the point of extinction.

The Humane Society of the United States makes a difference in the lives of animals here at home and worldwide. The HSUS is dedicated to creating a world where our relationship with animals is guided by compassion. We seek a truly humane society in which animals are respected for their intrinsic value, and where the human-animal bond is strong.

Want to help animals? We have plenty of suggestions. Adopt a pet from a local shelter, join The Humane Society and be a part of our work to help companion animals and wildlife. You will be funding our educational, legislative, investigative and outreach projects in the U.S. and across the globe.

Or perhaps you'd like to make a memorial donation in honor of a pet, friend or relative? You can through our Kindred Spirits program. And if you'd like to contribute in a more structured way, our Planned Giving Office has suggestions about estate planning, annuities, and even gifts of stock that avoid capital gains taxes.

Maybe you have land that you would like to preserve as a lasting habitat for wildlife. Our Wildlife Land Trust can help you. Perhaps the land you want to share is a backyard— that's enough. Our Urban Wildlife Sanctuary Program will show you how to create a habitat for your wild neighbors.

So you see, it's easy to help animals. And The HSUS is here to help.

2100 L Street NW • Washington, DC 20037 • 202-452-1100
www.hsus.org

DEDICATION

To my family.

TABLE OF CONTENTS

Chapter 3: Components of an Effective Estate Plan   59

Chapter 4: Taxes   79

Chapter 5: Wills   97

Chapter 6: Trusts   113

Chapter 7: Insurance   127

Chapter 8: Retirement Accounts   143

Chapter 9: Setting Priorities   159

Chapter 10: Choosing Who, What, How, When, and Why   173

Chapter 11: Planning Your Estate: Last Will and Testament in New York   187

Chapter 12: Keeping it Current   199

Conclusion   217

Appendix A: Estate-Planning Worksheets   219

Appendix B: New York Guardianship Court Forms   249

Appendix C: New York's Prudent Investor Act   259

Appendix D: Glossary of Terms   265

Bibliography   281

Biography   283

Index   285

INTRODUCTION

Estate Planning: What is It?

M any estate-planning books suggest you begin the process by taking inventory of all the possessions you will leave behind. This does make a certain amount of sense, as disposing of these things according to your wishes is indeed a part of estate planning. The problem is that simply comprising a list means you could end up with an extremely long list, including every single compact disc you own right now, not to mention the entire contents of your junk drawer — but to what end? You might have some idea of what matters to you right now, but what about five months or 50 years from now?

Asking difficult questions and understanding your priorities are the two most important parts of the estate-planning process. Whether you need a trust, additional life insurance, or a living will depends on what you want, not what a lawyer or an accountant tells you to do. Making such choices, though, can be difficult. Therefore, the first three chapters are designed to help you determine what you want.

Once you have a sense of the elements of estate planning that are important to you, then you have a reason to dig into the details about wills, beneficiaries, taxes, and all that other minutiae related to planning for whom you — not the courts or governments — want to benefit from your lifetime of hard work.

In this book, we provide a philosophy and common-sense approach to estate planning to give you a place to start. The first part of the book outlines a generalized overview of broadly applicable principles. As you will be reminded from time to time, several aspects of estate planning and provisions for your property at death are controlled by the laws of your state. *In Chapter 11, we focus on the specific requirements for New York residents.*

Throughout this book, you will see checklists, helpful tip boxes, and case studies by professionals or people in your similar situation to help you with the process of planning your estate. *Worksheets are provided in Appendix A.*

None of the information provided in this book is intended or should be interpreted to be legal advice. Each person's situation is unique and dependent on specific facts and circumstances. For legal advice specific to your situation, you must seek legal counsel from an attorney in your state who is specially trained or experienced in the field of estate planning and trusts.

CHAPTER 1

Getting Started

"Men in my family live well into their 70s, so I have plenty of time to do this."

"I created a will when my children were born. They are the only valuable 'possessions' I have, and they are already taken care of."

"This is only my third year in a full-time job. I have student loans to pay off and make no money. I do not have an estate to plan."

"We have been married for 12 years. If one of us dies before we get around to doing our estate planning, the spouse inherits everything — everyone knows that."

"Estate planning is for old people."

"I'll do it tomorrow."

These typical reasons and evasions for not doing any kind of estate planning are as varied and creative as the reasons concocted by children who did not do their homework. But unlike a teacher, who can excuse a missing paper, the state — the governmental body ultimately responsible for resolving all legal matters related to anything left behind by a person who has died — does not accept excuses from the next of kin: spouse, child, parents, or otherwise.

There are statutes that tell a judge how to distribute the ownership of real estate, pay credit card debts, satisfy mortgages, and assign cash, Grandma's antique end table, and the boxes of personal papers stashed in the attic. To make matters more confusing, each state has at least a slightly different idea about how the process must be handled, and Congress keeps changing the tax rules at the federal level.

According to estate-planning professionals, all the typical explanations for not doing estate planning are just excuses for avoiding two of the most taboo subjects in many cultures — money and death. With death comes feelings of fear, denial, and anger. With money comes the issue of self-worth, concern about the perceptions of others, and worries about the ability to support those who need help. These feelings and issues combine to create an emotional quagmire.

Pile on top of all that the unfamiliar terminology, complicated tax laws, and a host of people who have their hands out for a chunk of your estate and planning for what happens after your death is enough to cause anyone to exclaim, "The dog ate my estate plan."

Estate Planning Simplified

Like all complicated tasks, the best way to begin is to deal with individual pieces of information.

In simple terms, estate planning is the creation of a set of instructions about what should be done with your assets and personal belongings — money, possessions, investments, collectibles, and anything else you own — before and after you die. It is more than just writing a will that distributes your best china and savings accounts; it is more than writing a to-do list of things you want done, bills to pay, a good asking price for your house, or who you want to take care of your Fluffy, your collie.

Anyone who has possessions, no matter how many or how few, needs to have an estate plan. After you die, the mortgage payment still has to be made, and your favorite charity is still going to need the new roof or donation you pledged— but you will not be there to write the checks. The bank and the charity will express sympathy to your family, but they will be looking for the benefit of their commitment. Your family will not know how you want things handled if you have not left instructions, nor will they be bound to follow your wishes if you have not sealed them into legal documents.

This thing called estate planning is just a continuation of what you do now — sharing yourself, your money, and your life experiences with the people and organizations that are important to you. Estate planning allows you to make sure the money and property you accumulated during your life can continue to serve your purposes after you can no longer direct matters yourself.

You can do some things with your estate before you die, but there are other steps that cannot be taken until your death. There are technical aspects to consider, such as what taxes must be paid and how, in addition to distributing all your stuff. Before you can get to any of those details, you need to have an understanding of where you are in your life right now and the fact that it will end at some point.

Everyone Dies: A Simple Statement with Complicated Implications

Some people embrace a belief or philosophy that perceives death as a new adventure — the next step in living. Most people, though, do not see death, or even thinking about it, as fun or exciting. Thus, dying and all the trappings related to it rarely come up at the dinner table between "Pass the green beans," and "What's for dessert?" Given a choice between a conversation about death and clearing the dishes, people will fall over each other heading for the kitchen.

Like all things unfamiliar, the less death is discussed, the more taboo it becomes, and the more uncomfortable people feel when it does come up. Avoiding the subject of death and what happens to those who are left behind only makes it more frightening. Like learning mathematical equations or the periodic table of elements in chemistry, practice and repetition can demystify the unknown and put it in perspective.

Numerous books cover death and dying. As these books have increased in number and popularity, some basic knowledge has crept into everyday language and consciousness. Dr. Elisabeth Kubler-Ross, who wrote *On Death and Dying*, mainstreamed the acceptance of grief as a reasonable, human emotion. She used grief — the sad, gutwrenching feeling over losing someone loved or something cherished — to create a list of the emotional stages people experience when faced with a profound loss. These stages of grief have come to be embraced and recognized as normal and necessary in the human experience.

The Five Stages of Grief

1. **Denial and isolation.** Disbelief that the loss has taken place and possible withdrawal from familiar routines and people.

2. **Anger.** Feeling furious at the person who inflicted the hurt or at the world for letting it happen; upset with self for allowing the loss to occur, even if nothing could have stopped it.

3. **Bargaining.** Attempting to negotiate with a higher power, saying, "If I do this, will you change the outcome or bring about a miraculous solution?"

4. **Depression.** Feeling numb, lost, and unhappy. Anger and sadness may still be present.

5. **Acceptance.** All of the unsettled feelings calm down, maybe even fade, and the reality of the loss is finally acknowledged.

Even just imagining the loss of a loved one — as well as one's own death — can give rise to a semblance of these feelings. The advantage of facing these emotions is using the opportunity to face any self-doubt, fears, and anxiety that otherwise lurk either undetected or pushed beneath the events of day-to-day living.

Contemplating the inevitability of mortality need not be all doom and gloom, though. You can also use the process to think about the accomplishments, successes, and positive impacts you have had and expect to have. The estate-planning process can enable you to develop a more realistic view of yourself, your values, and the fruits of your efforts. The very act of planning empowers you to overcome any fears and worries about a seemingly dreary subject matter. You can also begin to see that even if you "cannot take it with you," the fruits of your labor have meaning and direction for you now.

Money Talk

Most adults do not want to include children in any discussion of financial issues because they see it as a burden or scary subject for their children. However, without age-appropriate participation in conversations about family finances, children will never be guided in their learning about the role and impact of money. An exclusionary approach turns money into an off-limits topic. It can also make money appear to be the cause of problems, a bad thing, or even a big secret. Even worse, it can be viewed as growing on trees.

By taking time to consider your past experiences with money, you can begin to understand the source of negative feelings or worries. You can also clarify in your mind the importance money has in your life right now. Decisions about the future are going to be difficult at best if you do not know what you want to accomplish — and disastrous if you make choices that are at odds with your true hopes and dreams or unrealistic for your circumstances.

One strong influence that can lead to misguided financial decisions is the proverbial "keeping up with the Joneses" mentality. Even if you do not think about painting your house to make it look as good as your neighbor's house that was just repainted, you most likely notice who has just re-painted their house, who has a new car, and who is going on an exotic vacation. The amount of disposable income someone has can create a materialistic link between net worth and self-worth.

A benefit of estate planning is getting a realistic grasp on your present circumstances as well as a developing concrete plan for the future.

I Do *What* with All This?

The point of giving serious thought to death and money is to sort through the mental and physical obstacles that cause you to put off estate planning.

To avoid feeling overwhelmed, or perhaps to feel you are accomplishing something "hands on," such as collecting bank records, consider using a practical, logical method for collecting and organizing potentially emotional and volatile memories, experiences, thoughts, and preliminary, basic documents.

Lists

Consider the topics that relate to you and your life situation — some suggestions are presented for you below. Create a list for each topic and organize the content into groups based on a common thread. Consider all possible angles for every topic, including past, present, and future. Be honest; nobody has to see your lists but you. For example:

Money

Memories — childhood/family

- Mom and Dad arguing about the mortgage at the end of every month

- Getting a piggy bank from Grandma and money every birthday to "save for college"

- Handing the bank teller my savings book and a bag of pennies, and she smiled at me when she gave me a sucker

- Having my own Christmas Club bank account

- Having an allowance and giving part of it to the family church, synagogue or favorite charity

Memories — adolescence

- Lemonade stand: math-class story problem turned Saturday afternoon project with friends, figuring out how to pay for ingredients and cups, how much to charge, and splitting the "profits" — I made my first dollar

- Being the only one who did not go on the class trip to Washington, D.C., because Dad was just laid off

- Working a summer job at a local grocery store

Adult experiences

- My first car dying on the freeway and having no money to tow it

- Getting that first student loan payment book after graduation

- Photocopying my first paycheck

- Overdrawing my checking account

- Paying my own rent and bills and having money left to send home

Dreams

- Owning my own home

- Paying for in-home care for Mom and Dad (so they do not have to live with me)

- Having three kids and sending them all to college

- Spending a year abroad before I die

- Not having to worry about paying bills every month (is that even possible?)

- Having enough capital to start my own business

Career versus job

Memories — childhood/family

- Work-ethic lectures from Grandpa while cleaning out the garage

- Grandma: "Put off work until tomorrow if you can play today"

- Uncle Jim who lived with us and never seemed to have a job

- Both Mom and Dad worked

Memories — adolescence

- Summer car wash for school fundraisers being hard work

- Career counselor at school being insisting my test scores meant I was going to be an engineer

- Wanting to dance in the school musical

- Quitting marching band to play football

Adult experiences

- Trying to make hobby of skateboarding into a business

- Intense dislike of all things entrepreneurial

- Feeling terrorized by bills

- Corporate downsizing

Dreams

- Have a job to make money to support the rest of my life

- Not owning so much stuff that I need a storage locker to hold it

- A job that means I can support a family and spend time with them

- Retiring at 50

Other topics to focus on can be death, family, career, play time/recreation, fears/worries, and anything else that evokes strong emotions as you consider other issues.

Journal

Choose a book with blank pages in which to record your estate-planning experience. Create sections for various stages in the process, leaving room for facts and figures, your feelings, and your thoughts. Leave space for doodling, notes, and pages of questions. Have pages for free association. For example, write "money" at the top of a page and write down what immediately comes to mind.

Stuff box

Find an old shoebox, or go out and buy something special for the estate-planning occasion. Put in your lists, thoughts scribbled on the back of a napkin while drinking coffee, and your journal. This gives you a dedicated place for all the planning bits and pieces, and documents when you need them no matter what the form. If a movie ticket stub reminds you of the film documentaries you want to make someday, toss it in.

File folders

If you need more structure in your life, create a folder each time you address a specific topic, including getting ready to do your estate planning. Choose a family photo or a picture from a magazine that illustrates what matters most to you, and tape or staple it into each folder. When you get frustrated or annoyed, look at those pictures to remind yourself of why the work is necessary.

Use index cards to jot down thoughts, or digitally record your musings while you commute to and from work or sit outside by yourself somewhere (porch, patio, yard, beach) — the method does not matter; it is doing the work that counts. Once you identify the factors that prevent you from planning for your death, you will be able to look more clearly at the present to help guide the future.

Here and Now

Beyond the tangle of complex emotions related to death and money, you need to figure out what is most important to you so that you can set some goals for what you want to happen after you die. How to go about doing that effectively depends on the individual and other people involved.

How one spouse views money can be dramatically different from how the other spouse's viewpoint. The people and things you each value may differ as well. What is valuable can be difficult to define because of the way culture seems to place high importance on materialistic things. Creating a personal values list is one way to begin identifying what matters most to you.

For example, some people might write, "Family matters most." However, there are also things necessary to survive — food, water, shelter, and medical care. These things are important, but that does not mean they represent a "value" that you hold. To distinguish these points, consider the following definitions:

- **Need**: A requirement; a necessity

- **Want**: To desire deeply; to wish for

- **Value**: To hold in high regard; to appreciate and rate highly; a moral view.

Once you can distinguish between your needs, wants, and values, consider the role that values play in your daily life. Those things that you value tend to serve as the test or measuring stick for making decisions.

When planning a summer vacation, do you feel it is more important to get away from daily stresses and relax in quiet with your immediate family, or is going on vacation without your parents and siblings never an option? Do you make sure you never miss extended-family events, such as weddings and graduations? You might value your extended family as highly as you do your immediate family, or your immediate family might be foremost in all decision-making. No one of these views is the "right" one. What is important is to understand which view is yours.

Stepping out of your everyday life to thoughtfully consider what makes up your everyday life is a way to gain perspective on what matters to you. Here are some matters to consider:

You

- Are you postponing something now, such as learning to paint, because you feel something else is more important, such as tutoring for your children?

- Are you a spiritual or religious person?

- Do you want your kids to have everything you did not?

- Is your decision-making impulsive or delayed by considered thought?

- Do you have time every day to do something you want to do? If not, why not?

Family

- How many children do you have or want to have? If you have children is possible you will have more some day, either by birth or adoption?

- What if infertility becomes an issue — do you want to adopt or consider other options?

- Are you close to your parents? Siblings? Other relatives?

- What role does extended family play in your life?

- Are there any relatives with whom you are particularly close?

- Are there relatives with whom you are estranged?

- Are there any family members who are missing, whereabouts unknown?

- Do you have children from a former marriage?

- Have you parented a child or children outside of legally recognized marriage?

Friends

- Are you close to people who are like family but not related by blood or marriage?

- Is "guys'/girls' night out/in" scheduled on a regular basis?

- Do you consult with one or more people about big changes you wish to make?

- Do you follow the advice of anyone in particular?

- Whom do you trust with your children when you are away?

Money

- What matters most to you — having enough money to pay the bills or having extra cash?

- Are you living paycheck to paycheck?

- How much money do you save from each paycheck?

- What retirement savings do you have, if any?

- How much debt do you have?

Community

- Is attending city council meetings a priority?

- Do you pick up trash when you are out walking the dog?

- When do you check a community calendar — when you are looking for a garage sale or trying to find something to do on a weeknight?

- Do you belong to a specific religious tradition to which you give your time and talents?

- When was the last time you chatted with a neighbor?

- Are you a member of any nonprofit boards?

- Do you volunteer for school or a charity?

The practical decisions to be made about your estate, such as who will get what, can gradually become clear as you sort out what is a feeling, what is important, and who is in your life. Instead of being caught up in whether the size of your estate will confirm your father's prediction that you would always be a screw-up, you can see how important he is to your family and that you want to do whatever you can to help care for him — before and after you die.

Separating facts from feelings will make it possible to see the opportunities and benefits that planning has to offer.

• *Did You Know?* •

At some point in time, most people have taken some kind of personality assessment test. In high school, they were designed to direct clueless teenagers toward a specific career path. Magazines claim to be able to identify your ideal mate based on a ten-question survey that identifies your personality based on the Myers-Briggs typology.

When assessments to be used in the workplace gained popularity in the 1980s, your human resources department might have rolled out a company-wide assessment program to help managers better understand and communicate with employees on a daily basis or to help them work through disputes. Lumped into one of four groups associated with a flavor of ice cream — "Are you a vanilla, too? Bo is a chocolate and Pat is a strawberry. No wonder my department is so messed up!" — the results seemed more gimmicky than informative and helpful.

Over time, research and development have refined and specialized these assessments to the point where the results provide surprisingly accurate, functional information about individual values and interests. If you are struggling with shifting priorities or feeling confused about how to deal with changes in your life, this is one tool that can offer some insight and direction.

Put This to Use

> If you have trouble creating a values list or putting into words what you feel is most important in your life, taking an assessment might help.
>
> Choosing an assessment tool can be difficult when you do not know where to look. The most reputable companies work with certified professionals — social workers, psychologists, coaches — whom they train to select the best assessment to provide the kind of information you need. The specialist will then talk through the results with you, asking questions and offering suggestions about how to use the results.
>
> TTI Success Insights® is an assessment company that offers an assessment called Personal Interests, Attitudes and Values ™. These assessments are not free, but the information they provide can be valuable.

What This Work Can Do

Change is difficult for most people on a good day, but under the influence of grief, it can be impossible to accomplish the most mundane tasks of cooking meals and taking out the garbage. At some point in the future, your family and close friends are going to be in that same position when dealing with your death.

Maybe your family will prefer to wear red, yellow, and bright orange to the memorial service. They might even make a family trip out of scattering your ashes on the Hudson River. Regardless of how your family will choose to cope with your death, there are steps you can take to allow them the freedom to do what they need to.

You can plan and pay for your funeral ahead of time. Perhaps you will be able to arrange to polish off the mortgage, make sure your mother's assisted-living bills are paid so she can spend her retirement money on cruises, add a new wing to the church, or set up a foundation to make sure your community council has an endowment for improved living conditions.

Estate planning can also help you now. By clarifying your priorities now, you can plan and save in ways that will allow you to realize your goals during your lifetime for your own pleasure and satisfaction as well as after you die. Estate planning can:

- Integrate and organize all your goals — personal, professional, financial, and estate

- Preserve your assets for use now and in the future

- Provide for your family and any chosen charities

- Ensure the efficient distribution of your estate the way you want it distributed

- Save money for your estate — taxes, legal fees, and court costs, for example

What Exactly is Involved

Each estate plan is different — and should be. Just as there are no two identical people in this context (even twins live their own lives), there are no one-size-fits-all estate plans. There are similar components, giving rise to numerous books about every possible aspect of estate planning. The subject also has generated its own complex body of law, giving rise to lawyers concentrating in this area and even specialty courts in many states.

Thus, depending on where you live, laws will affect what you can do with your property and when. This book is geared toward New York residents and the laws that come into play for those residents.

The chapters that follow assist you in the basic process of estate planning and suggestions for preparing to create your own estate plan. This, like any other book or template, ought to be a resource for gathering information and generating ideas. To adopt a canned plan that is sold as "cheap and easy" is to get what you pay for — not the outcomes you hope to achieve.

This book intends to help you do your homework and learn the terminology for asking questions of estate-planning professionals. If you want to do the job right, find people you can trust with your hopes and dreams and use them as the important resources they are.

As noted, what this book is not is a substitute for legal advice. We are providing general information to guide you in planning your personal estate plan. Laws change, and how they are applied depends on specific individual circumstances. When considering the application of statutes, always check to see whether they have changed. This can happen two ways. The state legislature might have amended a statute or Congress a federal statute. Courts also have the ability to affect how statutes work through judicial interpretation. These are additional reasons to utilize expert advice in the estate-planning process.

CASE STUDY: HIRING AN ESTATE-PLANNING COACH

Patricia Beaugard, Executive Coach
& Trainer
pat@patbeaugard.com
www.patbeaugard.com

Patricia Beaugard has extensive experience in the field of personal and professional coaching, in addition to being a trained ITT assessment specialist. She shares some of her thoughts on how a coach can be an important part of your estate-planning team.

Facing death

Many people have a difficult time facing the idea of their own death, so they avoid things that will remind them of it, like estate planning. Shifting the focus onto the people who are left behind, their survivors, is a way to focus on helping them. Ask, "What can I do to help my loved ones get through this difficult time in their lives?"

It can be helpful to look at what is bothering you: What is holding you back? What are your fears? All of these things indicate some underlying concerns; they might be related to dying, to money, or maybe to your family members. How much you will delve into these topics is based on individual preferences.

Making notes about your feelings and the thoughts that come up when you think about estate planning can be part of the process of identifying what you have, to whom it will be given, and how your possessions will be distributed. And it needs to be a process: Make some notes, then set it aside for a few days or weeks. Go back to it after you have had time to think about these things before you ask yourself, "Is this what I really want? Am I clear on this?"

Money, stuff, and meaning

Money represents something of value because of what it can be used for. Actually, it is a form of energy. Many people work hard for their money and are attached to it — they might struggle with the idea of "giving it away" to others because it represents their work and accomplishments.

For those who can see money as energy, it can flow to others because they can always get more.

People make decisions based on their emotions and their feelings. Sometimes they are not even aware of the feelings they have, so it can be helpful for another person to help them sort out those feelings. After you share your thoughts and feelings about a specific issue — like not wanting to distribute your estate — another person can share his or her impressions of your concerns. In that way, talking can help you explore how you feel and observe the influence those feelings have on your decision, or lack thereof.

Some people get quite passionate. That is when making time and space to step away and thoughtfully consider feelings and decisions is helpful; you can better determine whether that passion is a serious priority or a passing thing brought on by the estate-planning process. Consider:

- Where did this passion come from?
- Has this passion been a lasting influence?
- How have you lived this passion in your life?

I have a friend in Seattle who has never had children, but she has always had dogs, and all of them are rescued animals. For her vacation, she went to spend time with an organization in Utah that rescues all kinds of animals. She spent a week volunteering there, and she supports them financially. This is truly a value of hers because she supports it in word and deed.

Motivators and Values

By looking more deeply at what matters to you — your values — you will find what drives (or motivates) you to choose the profession you are in, where you live, or the kind of volunteer work you do for which organizations.

Another way to approach this is considering who and what is important in your life: extended family, non-blood "relatives," faith or spirituality, hobbies, the items you collect, or the traveling you do.

For people who have difficulty talking about or identifying these details, written assessments can help you determine your values in a concrete way. Do you care about making a difference in society? Not everyone does, but some people are quite driven by that. Are you focused on making sure your family has financial resources available to them, or do you value independence and want to foster that in your family? Maybe you see leaving your estate to your family as "spoiling" them.

What matters to you now might change in a few years — just look at the people or things you could never do without several years ago, and compare that to your life now. As a result, revisiting your motivators and values on a regular basis is important, and a coach can do more than remind you to take that second, third, and fourth look — she can ask you the questions you might forget to ask yourself so that your review is thorough.

Finding a coach

A life coach helps you look at and consider these complicated, difficult topics in a constructive manner. When choosing a coach, you want to decide what criteria are important to you. Do you want to work with a coach whom others have recommended? Do you want your coach to be certified? Do you want someone who has graduated from a coach-training program? What kind of background or experience is important in your eyes?

CHAPTER 2

Estate Planning Basics

According to a recent survey conducted by Harris Interactive:

- 55 percent of adult Americans do not have a will.

- 68 percent of adult African-Americans do not have a will.

- 74 percent of adult Hispanic-Americans do not have a will.

- 59 percent of adults do not have a living will.

- 62 percent of adults do not have a power of attorney for health care purposes.

- 10 percent of adults who have not prepared any part of an estate plan say it is because they do not wish to think about dying or becoming incapacitated.

- 9 percent of adults say they do not have an estate plan because they do not know who to talk to about creating one.

- 24 percent of adults say they have not created an estate plan because they lack the sufficient assets to require one.

The primary fact these numbers reveal is that most people do not plan for their deaths or what happens to their money and possessions once they are no longer around to call the shots. The reasons are very likely among those discussed in the previous chapter and more. Certainly, many people view estate planning either as complicated, frightening or only for the very rich.

But estate planning is neither mysterious nor incomprehensible. It certainly is not a privilege reserved for the wealthy. Everyone can have a will. Everyone can plan for the future.

Even though estate planning does encompass a broad array of potentially complicated issues, such as federal tax law and boilerplate legal language required by the courts, you do not need to become an expert in all these areas to have a valid will and an estate plan. The most important thing to recall is the simple foundation on which all of this rests: When you die, your property stays here. You have a right to speak about what happens with these things.

Of course, you can be buried with your platinum credit card or favorite jewelry, and you might even be able to arrange to be buried in your car, but the taxes and balance due on debts or liabilities must be paid and the rest of your property must go somewhere; your spouse and children, if you have them, might have legal claims — all these considerations are part of your estate.

Suppose you want your son to have your house and you give him the keys. Sounds like "possession," right? Everyone one has heard the old saying, "possession is 9/10 of the law." So will this not work? Unfortunately, your son cannot claim to own the family house simply by saying, "She gave me the keys before she died and said it is mine." If you do not transfer the title to his name by executing the necessary legal documents with the required legal formalities, then legally, the house is still yours. If you have not named him as beneficiary in your will, and you have other heirs besides your son, or you have creditors who claim the house for payment, then your son is not likely to get it.

Without doing the necessary legal paper work, your belongings are still your belongings — your debts and your assets — and if you die without a will, the state will dispose of all of it according to law because you are no longer around to do it yourself.

Beyond the material items are the unexpected and potentially more complicated issues leading up to your death. A heart attack or car accident could result in brain death or a coma. Who makes the decision about your medical care and the use of extraordinary means to extend your life?

The best way to ensure that your wishes are carried out is to make them known in such a way that there is no doubt about what they are. That means learning the facts about what you can and cannot do and how to ensure what you can do will be followed.

Debunking Myths

People will do, say, and believe just about anything to avoid doing things they do not want to do; estate planning is no exception. Perhaps this is how so many myths have developed about death and taxes.

- **Myth: The estate tax — the "death tax" — was repealed, so there are no taxes to avoid anymore**. The federal estate tax law was repealed for one year at the beginning of 2010, according to a law called the Economic Growth and Tax Relief Reconciliation Act, enacted in 2001. If you happen to die during 2010, then your estate will not have to pay federal estate taxes, but it will still be subject to any estate taxes that may be imposed by New York. The estate tax comes back in 2011, according to the same law — unless Congress makes more changes. *There will be more information about taxes in Chapter 4.*

- **Myth: All I need is a will — it will take care of all of my assets**. Debts do not go away; even if a will sets aside money to pay those debts, it might not be sufficient. In that case, the assets in your estate, such as your grandchild's college fund perhaps, will be tapped to pay creditors. Additionally, a will only addresses property that is in your name — meaning your name is the only one listed on the title as the owner. Property that is owned jointly with survivorship rights or pay-on-death (POD) beneficiaries — such as real estate, retirement accounts, or life insurance policies — will pass to the surviving owner or go to a beneficiary. *Chapter 5 goes into more detail about wills in general, and Chapter 11 speaks specifically to New York wills.*

- **Myth: Trusts are for wealthy people**. A trust can be created by anyone who has an asset or assets to make the subject (the res) of the trust. A trust can eliminate or dramatically reduce the amount of estate taxes that will be paid by your survivors and/or your estate, if it is set up properly during your lifetime. Choosing the right kind of trust to suit your needs and applying careful adherence to legal language will make a trust a viable option for anyone. Chapter 6 further addresses trusts.

- **Myth: Life insurance is not subject to estate tax, so I do not need to do any other planning**. Life insurance proceeds frequently are not subject to income tax if they are paid to someone else, like a spouse, parents, or a charitable institution. However, if you own a life insurance policy and you have not named a beneficiary, then the proceeds of that policy become part of your estate and will be subject to state and federal estate tax. Any person who receives the insurance proceeds will likely receive those proceeds without incurring any income tax liability unless it is in a state that makes it subject to inheritance tax. Also, a beneficiary of insurance proceeds where the beneficiary has paid the premiums might be taxed on the proceeds minus the amount of the premiums paid. *Chapter 7 elaborates on insurance.*

- **Myth: If I do not name a beneficiary for my 401(k), my spouse still gets the money**. Assets that do not have a named beneficiary in a will or some other legal document will end up in probate court as part of your estate. This might benefit your spouse, or it might not. If you want your spouse or some other person to receive the unused portion of any retirement savings accounts, then they must be named as a beneficiary. Naming a second, or backup, beneficiary will also keep the account out of probate if the primary beneficiary is already deceased or declines the gift for some reason. *Including your retirement accounts into your estate plan is covered in Chapter 8.*

- **Myth: If I die without a will, my spouse gets everything**. In some states, this is true; in others, it is not. The laws of the state in which you live at the time of your death will determine who gets what, and creditors will be paid first. For example, in New York, if you own real property in two or more states — maybe a condo in Florida, a house in New York, and a cottage in Michigan — the courts of each state will be involved in the distribution of these assets. *The court's involvement with your estate is further explained in Chapter 11.*

The list of misinformation or partial truths continues, with no signs of stopping. As estate tax laws change to close loopholes or take advantage of new revenue opportunities, the areas you think you already know about estate planning will become obsolete without your knowledge. Over time, most people buy and sell components such as houses and stock portfolios, and those changes mean that an estate is a changeling, too. Whether your estate is growing or diminishing, you need to know what you have, how it changes, and how you want it to be handled after your death.

Your Estate

Yes, you have one, and defining it will most likely be the most straightforward part of this entire process. Your estate is made up of everything you own, or your entire net worth stated numerically.

The formula for figuring out your net worth — a person's true financial value — is simple:

$$\text{Assets - Liabilities = Net Worth}$$

Asset: Anything a person owns or is owed; this can be money, real estate, investments, or any other tangible property.

Liability: A debt or an obligation to pay money to another person or institution; also called a negative balance.

Following are some examples of common assets and liabilities comprising an estate:

Assets

- Annuities
- Cars
- Cash
- Certificates of deposit
- Insurance
- Investments
- Personal property (jewelry, stamp collection, or household items, for example)
- Real estate
- Rental income
- Retirement funds
- Savings/checking accounts

- Stock certificates
- Structured settlements (lottery winnings or lawsuit settlements, for example)

Liabilities

Bills/debts:

- Alimony
- Automobile payments
- Child support
- Credit card balances
- Future debt (a child's college tuition or care of parents, for example)
- Student loans
- Insurance premiums
- Mortgages (first- and second-home equities)
- Personal loans
- Taxes

Because it is important to keep your list of assets up-to-date, you might consider using a digital camera to make a visual inventory of your assets so that you can create an archive of these items. When documenting a dollar value for each, such as the appraisal of a necklace, you can scan that appraisal and make it part of the electronic archive. You can also collect and scan any other documents, such as stock certificates, purchase invoices, or a house deed.

These documents will be essential when meeting with estate-planning advisors, so collecting them in a secure, fireproof safe as you build your inventory will save time later.

People

You never know how many friends you have until you win the lottery; the same can be true about your death. Some people never know how many creditors, lost family, and illegitimate children they supposedly had until their will is made part of the public record. After your death is legally certified, your will must be filed with the court, in which it becomes public record. Anyone who wants to make a claim against your estate can do so, and that is when the real work begins for those who helped you with your planning.

To make sure your wishes are understood and carried out, you need to make sure that the people who are connected with your estate planning do as you choose, not what is most convenient for them.

Paid professional planners and those who carry out your wishes, such as executors, secondary executors, or legal guardians — and others — such as the court, creditors, and beneficiaries — will have a say in what happens after you are gone. Some people are outside your control, such as the court judge and unforeseen claimants, but you can choose those who will serve as the representatives who manage your estate.

Estate-planning professionals

Yes, there are people who actually enjoy estate-planning work. What might seem like torture to you is a challenging, rewarding career for someone who likes helping people sort out and plan for the future. The fees they charge can be an hourly rate, a per-document fee, or an ongoing estate-management fee. Be sure you understand what the charges are and how they are paid — and, if there is a contract, read the fine print.

Lawyer

Also called attorneys, lawyers can specialize in specific aspects of estate planning, such as wills, trusts, or probate procedure, or they might have a broader focus, such as estate planning or tax law. Depending on the size of your estate, you might need to consult with more than one lawyer to make sure all the legal issues related to your estate are properly prepared for. Some law firms have multiple members who can do all your work in-house under the direction of your lead lawyer. Or, you might feel more comfortable having different firms work on different parts of your estate plan. No matter how you approach this, you need to be forthcoming about all your personal goals and estate-planning wishes with everyone involved so that the work on the various areas support, not undermine or contradict each other.

Certified public accountant (CPA)

Accountants can specialize in various aspects of financial estate matters such as trusts, annuities, and estate tax law, but they also serve as estate-planning specialists who can help you consider all financial decisions. An accountant must be current on tax law and other legal requirements related to accounting for money. Like a law firm, an accounting firm might have several people on staff who specialize in different areas. However, the same caution applies: Be comfortable with your CPA, because he or she has to be trusted with all the same personal information if he or she is going to work well with the others on your team.

Financial planner

There are all kinds of financial planners out there with initials after their names, such as Certified Financial Planner® (CFP®), Chartered Financial Analyst (CFA), and some without initials. But all of them analyze a person's overall financial situation and develop a comprehensive plan in conjunction with the individual, designed to meet his or her financial goals and objectives. Certified planners have followed a specific course of education or training classes, and some go on to develop expertise in specific areas such as estate or retirement planning. Financial planners can help you prepare your estate to achieve a target goal for a certain age or projected time of death value that you want to leave behind. Be wary of anyone who is self-taught or who works on 100 percent commission — the advice you get might not necessarily be based on the most current information or in your best interest. Commissioned sales people have an interest in selling specific products to earn their livelihood, which will not necessarily coincide with your needs or your pocketbook.

Insurance agent

Gone are the days when an insurance sales person appeared at your door and offered to spend hours chatting with you about your insurance needs — home, auto, and life being the basics. Today, many representatives go through human resources departments to communicate long-term and short-term disability coverage for company employees, which might or might not be partially paid for by the employer. Medical and dental insurance — not to mention pet insurance, long-term care insurance, and other less common insurance plans — are now sold over the phone or on the Internet. An actual insurance agent can help you with your estate planning by assessing the kind and amount of insurance you need and can afford. A real agent, rather than a call-center staffer, is the better person to speak to your insurance needs, but if you cannot find one, your other estate-planning professionals might be able to help.

Coaches

Financial, professional, and personal coaches can help you identify and manage monetary, career, and personal goals. At a time when mixed messages about being loyal to your employer and diversifying your stock portfolio make you wonder what you ought to do about the stock options your company offers, a coach can help you sort out the implications of selling or keeping those options and the potential impact on your career and estate plan. Their goal is to see you succeed, not make sure a corporation thrives or your beneficiaries get a chunk of change. A coach is an objective third party who, at the same time, is hired to focus primarily on what is best for you. There are certification courses for various forms of coaching, but there are no national standards, and formal training is not required to present oneself as a coach. This means you must ask some specific questions about the person's experience, training, and references.

Spiritual advisor

The altruistic efforts of many people are based on their chosen faith traditions or their own moral compasses. Some types of difficult decisions about personal matters are not always accounting or purely legal issues. For example, you might be trying to decide whether your drug-addicted brother will be helped or hurt by a large inheritance as part of your estate plan. Choosing charitable institutions to benefit from your life's work might be another consideration. Changes in your life such as divorce or the unexpected death of a loved one might necessitate changes in your will at a time when the family member you would normally discuss those things with is grieving. A minister, priest, rabbi, or other faith consultant can offer guidance, support, and information related to your belief system that might be helpful in these situations. Someone to talk to about personal matters related to family decisions especially speaks to the values and priorities you have identified early in the estate planning process.

Whether you need any or all of these people in their various roles to participate in your estate plan is up to you and the types of issues that bother you about the process. Though some do not charge anything, others might have flat rates or hourly charges. The money you invest, much like the time you invest, is valuable, so be sure you weigh the short-term costs against the long-term gains.

If your choice is utilizing more than one person to assist your planning, consider choosing one person to serve as the primary contact through which all information will flow. If you choose a lawyer to serve as your point person (usually the best choice), he or she would work with the other professionals on your team to collect and ask for clarification about their part of your estate management. Then he or she would meet with you and, at one time, go through all the information. A time-saving efficiency for you, this will cost a little extra because you need to pay your lawyer to do this coordination work, but in the long run, you will have a reliable, well-informed person who can serve in your stead when you are gone and someone who understands the complete picture of your estate and your intentions.

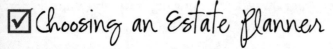
☑ Choosing an Estate Planner

Estate planner qualities and characteristics:

Qualifications for estate-planning professionals will vary based on their professional focus and expertise. Individual training is important, but there are some fundamental skills that all of them ought to have. Scrutinize prospective estate-planning team members before and after you meet with them — they will be privy to your most personal and private information

Before: Do some homework before you meet with a planner.

☐ **Is your estate planner ethical?** Check with the Better Business Bureau and any related professional organizations, such as the American Bar Association for lawyers, to find out whether any complaints have been filed or reprimand proceedings have taken place.

☐ **How well does your planner interact with clients?** Get references for current clients to inquire about the positives and negatives of working with this person. Some questions to ask his or her current clients might be:

– Is this person prepared for meetings, and does he or she follow-through on tasks that need to be done afterward?

    – How well does this person collaborate with other estate-planning professionals?

    – Do you spend much time in the waiting area before an appointment?

    – Have you ever had mistakes occur with your invoices?

    – Have your meetings ever been canceled on short notice?

☐ **What professional associations is your planner a part of?** If this person is the member of an organization, call and inquire about his or her involvement and whether the organization can make any referrals.

☐ **What services does your planner offer?** Find out the range of services this person offers, or whether he or she works in collaboration with others inside or outside his or her company.

☐ **Is your planner considerate?** Being willing to listen to your concerns and needs is essential; review his or her Web site or any promotional materials for signs of this trait.

After: When you meet with an estate-planning professional for the first time, pay attention to the level of comfort or discomfort you feel, and evaluate that meeting soon after. These are a few questions to consider:

☐ Did he or she ask you relevant questions?

☐ Which did he or she do more, talk or listen?

☐ Did he or she tell you what you should do, or present you with options to consider?

☐ Did he or she disclose any commissions or other considerations he or she receives from the institutions offering the products he or she represents? For example, he or she presents three different kinds of life insurance; for one of those, he or she will receive a commission if you sign on the dotted line.

☐ Did he or she explain things in a way that you could understand?

☐ Was he or she willing to go back over details until you were clear about confusing points?

☐ Were you given fees and hourly rates in writing?

☐ Are you expected to sign a contract?

☐ Were you given a timeline or some other expectation about how long this process might take?

☐ Did you feel you were being helped, or seen as nothing more than a revenue stream?

CASE STUDY: WHAT IT TAKES
TO BE A FINANCIAL ADVISER

U.S. Department of Labor
Bureau of Labor Statistics
www.dol.gov

Estate planning is a specialty within the field of financial planning, and the U.S. Department of Labor, via the Bureau of Labor Statistics, predicts this is going to be a growth industry for many years to come.

Beyond that, the bureau also provides job descriptions and other information about various industries, including financial advisers and planners. This material provides a description of the kind of work a planner might do in a day and the characteristics of a person who is successful in this kind of position. You might not be looking to make a career change, but this can serve as excellent background material when you begin looking for an estate planner to help you develop your plan.

Financial analysts

Significant points:

- Most personal financial advisers have a bachelor's degree.
- Math, analytical, and interpersonal skills are important.
- Keen competition is anticipated for these highly paid positions, despite much faster than average job growth.
- About 29 percent of personal financial advisers are self-employed.

Nature of the work:

Personal financial advisers assess the financial needs of individuals and assist them with investments, tax laws, and insurance decisions. Advisers help their clients identify and plan for short-term and long-term goals. Advisers help clients plan for retirement, education expenses, and general investment choices. Many also provide tax advice or sell insurance. Although most planners offer advice on a wide range of topics, some specialize in areas such as retirement and estate planning or risk management.

Education and training:

A bachelor's or graduate degree is strongly preferred for personal financial advisers. Employers usually do not require a specific field of study for personal financial advisers, but a bachelor's degree in accounting, finance, economics, business, mathematics, or law provides good preparation for the occupation. Courses in investments, taxes, estate planning, and risk management are also helpful.

Licensure:

Personal financial advisers who directly buy or sell stocks, bonds, insurance policies, or specific investment advice need a combination of licenses that varies based upon the products they sell. In addition to those licenses, smaller firms that manage clients' investments must be registered with state regulators, and larger firms must be registered with the Securities and Exchange Commission. Personal financial advisers who choose to sell insurance need licenses issued by State boards.

Other qualifications:

Personal financial advisers need strong math, analytical, and interpersonal skills. They need strong sales ability, including the ability to make a wide-range of customers feel comfortable. Personal financial adviser training emphasizes the different types of investors, and how to tailor advice to the investor's personality. They need the ability to present financial concepts to clients in easy-to-understand language. Some advisors have experience in a related occupation, such as accountant, auditor, insurance sales agent, or broker.

Financial Analysts

Significant points:

- Financial analyst positions require a bachelor's or master's degree.
- Positions may also require professional licenses and certifications.
- Keen competition is anticipated for these highly paid positions.
- Financial analysts earn high wages.

Nature of the work:

Financial analysts provide guidance to businesses and individuals making investment decisions. Financial analysts assess the performance of stocks, bonds, commodities, and other types of investments. Also called securities analysts and investment analysts, they work for banks, insurance companies, mutual and pension funds, securities firms, the business media, and other businesses, making investment decisions or recommendations.

Education and training:

A bachelor's or graduate degree is required for financial analysts. Most companies require a bachelor's degree in a related field, such as finance, business, accounting, statistics, or economics. An understanding of statistics, economics, and business is essential, and knowledge of accounting policies and procedures, corporate budgeting, and financial analysis methods is recommended. An MBA or a master's degree in finance is often required. Advanced courses or knowledge of options pricing, bond valuation, and risk management are important.

Licensure:

The Financial Industry Regulatory Authority (FINRA) is the main licensing organization for the securities industry. Depending on an individual's work, different licenses may be required, although buy side analysts are less likely to need licenses. The majority of these licenses require sponsorship by an employer, so companies do not expect individuals to have these licenses before starting a job.

Other qualifications:

Strong math, analytical, and problem-solving skills are essential qualifications for financial analysts. Good communication skills are necessary because these workers must present complex financial concepts and strategies. Self-confidence, maturity, and the ability to work independently are important. Financial analysts must be detail-oriented, motivated to seek out obscure information, and familiar with the workings of the economy, tax laws, and money markets. Although much of the software they use is proprietary, financial analysts must be comfortable working with spreadsheets and statistical packages.

Who Will Carry Out Your Wishes in Your Place?

At the heart of estate planning is the recognition that at some point in time, you are going to die, and before then, you might become incompetent. When that happens, someone else must take responsibility for your estate. This responsibility will involve both people and property.

Determining who will serve as the legal guardian of minor children is a huge decision and a tremendous responsibility for the person/people who agree/s to be responsible for the health and well-being of your children. A guardian of a minor — any adult legally appointed to be responsible for the needs of your children until they reach legal age — is not the same as a guardian for an adult. The guardian of an adult is any adult who can be legally appointed to manage the affairs of an incompetent or infirm adult of any age. A mentally challenged 32-year-old brother can need a guardian as much as a parent in the early stages of Alzheimer's disease.

Equally important is the executor of your estate. An executor, also called a personal representative, is the individual who handles the property you are leaving behind. If you die without a will, the court appoints an administrator — frequently a spouse or adult child. This person's fiduciary obligation is to make sure your assets and liabilities are disposed of in a legal, efficient, and thoughtful manner. The money necessary to support your children, a disabled sibling, or your aging parents will be in the hands of your executor.

Legal guardians

Whether for a child or an adult, appointing the guardianship of another person is legal action. The court might appoint a guardian based on the wishes of the person making the request, if the appointment is determined to be in the best interest of the child. A child's godparents do not automatically become guardians upon your death; you should put guardianship in writing in a will or, in New York, through appointment of a standby guardian. If you are the legal guardian of your elderly mother, you need to make provisions for her care in your will or by other legal proceedings in the event that you might die before she does.

The guardian for a minor will be responsible for items like food, clothing, and shelter. However, he or she also might be responsible for managing assets in the child's name and providing for things such as education and health care. The same can be true for the guardian of an adult, who might also be responsible for paying bills and making sure the home is cleaned on a regular basis.

Choosing any guardian is difficult because of the responsibilities involved. The most obvious concern is selecting someone who will care for your family the way you would, but more important is whether the person will follow through on the commitment. A person in her 20s in the midst of building a career might say she is willing to set aside her career to care for her sister's young children, but after three years, will she still be willing to stay at home with the kids, even though money is not an issue?

New York's form for appointment of a standby guardian in the family court and other guardianship forms are included in the Appendices of this book. These forms are provided for informational purpose. It is advised they be used only with assistance of legal counsel.

Consider some of the following:

- **Age**: Young and old are as much about experience as birth date. Do you want the person taking care of your children to be your same age?

- **Lifestyle**: Your sister is non-religious, but you want your children to attend a Catholic church. Will she take them to church every Sunday?

- **Child-rearing/caring-for-adult skills**: Patience is essential, as is the savvy to know where to find and seek help as needed. Is the person you are considering good with kids?

- **Marital status**: Your divorced brother is fabulous with your boys, but would two parents be better for your children? Would your sister and her husband be better?

- **Compatibility**: If your kids hate your sister's husband, this is not going to be a good long-term fit. How do your kids respond to the person you are considering?

- **Money skills**: Your aunt is a penny pincher, but your uncle is a spendthrift. Will the money set aside for your brother's group-home bills be well conserved under their watch?

You also need to consider your expectations for your children and how much of those you want to impose on the people who will become their guardians. Once you come up with the priorities you have for your children, make a list of several people and ask each of them whether they would be willing to serve as guardians under the conditions that you lay out. It is a bad idea to name someone as guardian without her knowledge. If she refuses, the court will then decide what is in the best interest of the minors or others in need of care. The people the court chooses might not be to your liking.

A secondary or "backup" guardian will address the gap left by people who might be unable to serve in that capacity.

• *Did You Know?* •

A property guardian or property manager is a legal adult who takes responsibility for the oversight of property inherited by a minor/child. Children under the age of 18 can inherit property, but they are only allowed to legally own that property with adult supervision; an adult must have the responsibility of managing it. Just because a 17-year-old can inherit a car does not mean he or she is "in charge."

The responsibility of becoming the legal guardians of a minor child or children might be enough for the people you select to provide for their upbringing. If the burden of managing their property on top of that is too much, another person can be appointed for that role.

Put This to Use

Harry and Sally set up an education trust for their three minor children — Huey, Dewy, and Louis — in addition to putting the house and all other assets in their names. They are enrolled in private schools and will continue to live in their home; Aunt Blanche is moving in with them.

Blanche has a good heart but is bad with money — so bad that she forgets to make her own house payment. Putting her in charge of making sure the tuition is paid from the proper accounts and the property taxes are paid on time is a disaster waiting to happen. So, Harry and Sally named their long-time banker and trust officer, Bill Smith, as the property manager. He also knows Blanche, so she can easily call him to ask for help if any additional school fees need to be paid. This frees her to focus on the boys instead of on the finances.

An added bonus is that Bill, as a trust officer for a bank, is not likely to get away with embezzling money from the trusts. Bill cannot be paid a fee, which means more money for the trust.

☑ Choosing a Guardian

You, your children, a sibling, or a parent might one day need another person to make decisions that you — or they — would normally make. Asking someone else to take on your responsibilities in addition to their own is a significant request that carries legal, ethical, and moral implications. This is a brief list of details to consider when making a list of people you might want to ask to serve in this capacity:

☐ **Eligibility:** Different states have different procedures, though the best interest of the child is the primary directive. New York's procedure is governed by family court. *The forms in Appendix B show how basic information is presented to the court for official appointment of guardians.* Court appointment of a standby guardian for future application is an advisable procedure to have a guardian in place for minor children or other dependents.

☐ **Common ideals:** People who have similar views about child rearing, values, and religious beliefs are more likely to raise your children or care for your adult family members in the way that you would.

☐ **Compassionate:** There could be a need to address the emotional and practical issues and needs that come up as a result of your death.

☐ **Flexible:** Different people react differently to dramatic changes in life, so it might be necessary for the guardian to take time off work or move to a new home to be available to address the needs of his charge.

☐ **Emotional stability:** Grief is a reasonable response to death, but a person who is prone to depression or has mental health issues might not be able to care for others during such a critical time.

☐ **Marital status:** Some people prefer that children have a two-parent family; others are more focused on the personality of the guardian, and maybe being single means being more flexible. Consider what is most important to you, and be true to that criterion.

☐ **Location:** : If the guardian is unable to move into your home or be close to his or her adult charge, those entrusted to them might have to move, and that could create additional stresses for already-stressed people.

Things to keep in mind...

- Some family members might not be happy with your choice of guardian or might believe they are the best choice. Be prepared to address fears, concerns, and frustrations — even anger — with those who disagree with your choices.

- *Always* discuss the expectations and responsibilities with the potential guardian before naming that person in a will or other legal document.

  ▶ If it makes you both feel more comfortable, spell out your expectations for each guardian in writing so that you are both clear about your wishes.

- *Always* choose secondary and tertiary guardians in the event that unexpected situations (your first choice dies before you do) or life circumstances (serious illness or a job transfer to another country) make it impossible for that person to agree to be a guardian.

- Be aware that the court might decide that your choices for a guardian might not be suitable — maybe your brother was recently arrested on drunken-driving charges — and choose another guardian based on what the judge thinks is in the best interest of the child or person in need of a guardian. This is where naming secondary and tertiary guardians can be helpful in guiding the court..

Executor

Just as you need to carefully select your guardians, you need to consider who will manage the affairs of your estate, as opposed to running off to the Cayman Islands with everything in your trust funds.

See Chapter 5 for more information on the responsibilities of an executor. The following list offers a quick summary of his or her duties:

- Guiding your will through the probate process to make sure it is accepted as valid. This also means defending the will against any challenges.

- Collecting your assets.

- Overseeing the transition of gifts made to beneficiaries. This might include a title transfer for a house or making sure a life insurance policy check is made out in the correct name.

- Reviewing, evaluating, and paying any claims against your estate. These commonly include taxes and outstanding bills that are owed.

- Raising the money to pay claims. This can mean selling assets, such as a house or car.

- Preparing and filing an accounting of all financial transactions for the court.

The person who takes on this task must know what is involved. For this reason, choosing a secondary executor is a good idea; if you do not appoint one, the court will appoint one for your estate.

☑ Choosing an Executor or Trustee

The choice of an executor or a trustee is a highly personal decision, so there is no cookie-cutter definition or approach. Some details to consider are:

☐ **Integrity:** Can you trust this person, no matter what?

☐ **Your relationship:** Does this person know you well enough personally and professionally to know how you think and might want things handled?

☐ **Personality:** How will this person deal with a grieving family when decisions must be made?

☐ **Thoughtfulness:** Will this person consider questions and demands made on your estate by creditors, beneficiaries, the court, or anyone contesting your will and wishes?

☐ **Common sense:** When given multiple choices, does this person tend to be practical?

☐ **Realism:** If this person does not know what to do, will he or she seek the advice of experts?

☐ **Potential conflict of interest:** Could decisions made by this person benefit others, including your trustee/executor, and harm your family?

☐ **Asset management skills:** What kind of experience does this person have with real estate and financial markets, for example?

☐ **Real estate management skills:** Is this person informed about what it takes to maintain and manage property in your estate, be it a house or undeveloped piece of land?

☐ **Knowledge of beneficiaries:** Can this person accurately assess the needs of your beneficiaries without your day-to-day guidance?

☐ **Criminal background:** Has this person ever been convicted of a crime related to the responsibilities you are asking of him or her?

Additional considerations/notes: _____

_____

_____

_____

People of Influence

After you are gone, the people who will have the most influence over what happens to your estate, in the legal pecking order, are the probate court, creditors, and your beneficiaries.

Probate court judge

The following contains information about how the court operates. *Specifics about how probate court accepts, records, and addresses issues with wills are addressed in Chapter 11.*

Probate court is part of a state's court system; some states have special judges who only handle estate settlement cases, whereas others might not specialize in that way. New York has a unified court system. The surrogate court, which is a court of general jurisdiction, handles probate matters; family court handles guardianship.

Regardless of the laws governing the organizational structure of the court, a probate judge will review the legal documents related to an estate. If a person dies without a will, the judge will appoint an administrator who serves in the same capacity as an executor. He or she also will ask for and review details such as the will (if there is one), the inventory of assets, and petitions from creditors and heirs. Heir is the legal title of a person who inherits property from an estate that does not have a will, or is intestate; beneficiaries are those who receive an inheritance by being named in a legal document such as a will or trust.

The judge will supervise the process of settling your estate and will only adjudicate, or hand down decisions, as they are needed, such as when a creditor makes a claim and is denied payment by the administrator. The same can be done when a person comes forward and claims to be an heir to your estate.

The judge might choose someone you think is unsuitable for the job of administrator, and he or she might agree to pay the claim of an old business partner whom you do not feel you owe. You can prevent these items from happening by creating an estate plan and avoiding probate when possible.

Probate judges also establish guardianship and handle other special circumstances, such as bigamy, live-in lovers who want part of an estate, or "long-lost children" who contest decisions regarding heirs.

Creditors

Your debts are paid first, so how much you owe other people at the time of your death will determine how much of your estate goes to your loved ones and charities. Some creditors might not make a claim against your estate.

Maybe you borrowed $5,000 from Aunt Henrietta and she does not care about being paid back, so when your executor writes a check, she simply tears it up and hands it back.

Outstanding credit card balances, a personal line of credit from a bank, and a car loan are just a few examples of the bills you might be paying when you are alive, and these must be settled after your death. In addition to letting creditors know about your passing, your executor will request the amount of payments necessary to settle your accounts. Some companies, upon reading a death notice, might try to make a claim of payments due. It is up to the executor or administrator — or the probate judge, if this becomes necessary — to determine whether a claim is legitimate and must be paid.

Beneficiaries

Even if you die intestate, which means to die without leaving a will, there are a number of will substitutes that make it possible for your estate to avoid probate completely: joint ownership of property, wherein the surviving partner automatically takes full control; revocable and irrevocable trusts; life insurance, pensions, and annuities with named beneficiaries; and stocks, bonds, and bank accounts paid to a designated person upon the death of the owner.

If a beneficiary is not named — or the primary beneficiary declines the bequest, or is dead and a secondary beneficiary is not named — then the probate court judge will decide who receives the unclaimed property.

Beneficiaries and court-named heirs can challenge decisions made about an inheritance — whether you or the court makes that decision. People who believe they ought to have received an inheritance or who only received a fraction of what they were told they would get — or think they deserve — can challenge the will or court ruling. These challenges can hold up the resolution of your estate for months or years, so making sure your legal documents are in order can help reduce this problem.

These basic elements of an estate plan describe what is involved and who is integral to the process. Next are the components of an estate plan — the documents, accounts, and policies that make it all legal and taxable.

CASE STUDY: DETAILS AND LEGALESE DO MATTER

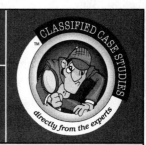

Scott M. Slovin, Esq.
Schwartz Manes Ruby & Slovin
sslovin@smrslaw.com
www.smrslaw.com

What are some estate plan essentials?

The biggest concern in an estate plan is coordinating all of the estate plan documents, such as the will, with the trust and beneficiary designations, as well as ownership of assets, including payable-on-death or transfer-on-death-type assets. Essential information includes the following:

- The name of the testator (the person preparing the will) or the grantor or settlor (the name of the person creating the trust) of the trust.
- Beneficiaries' names and relationships to the testator or the grantor as well as alternate (contingent) beneficiaries, should a beneficiary predecease the testator or grantor.
- The fiduciaries (the executor or trustee) and the guardians for the minor children.
- How estate taxes and other expenses of the estate will be paid and from which assets the cash will be drawn.

The benefits of working with an attorney are to avoid mistakes in drafting — such as unclear bequests or failure to specify from what assets taxes will be paid — and to reduce federal and state estate taxes that a non-estate-planning lawyer or a non-attorney might fail to take into consideration.

Why is it important to use legal terms in estate-planning documents? So many of them are confusing.

There is a long history of interpretation under state law and federal tax law, and attorneys like to use language that they know has been interpreted by the courts to achieve the results they are seeking for clients. Attorneys are trying to simplify their language and create wills and trusts that are easier to read and for clients to follow.

How does a person go about choosing a professional in your field?

The best way to choose an estate-planning attorney is to seek the recommendation of financial planners, accountants, and insurance agents who work with estate-planning attorneys. Make sure you choose someone who does more than a couple of wills per year. You need to find someone who spends at least half of the time in estate planning so that he understands all of the nuances of state probate and estate law, as well as tax law. Especially important would be attorneys who have extra training in the field of estate planning and tax planning. Recommendations of friends and neighbors would also be important.

CHAPTER 3
Components of an Effective Estate Plan

C ar keys, directions, map, water bottle, and snacks: Planning for a road trip is easy because the basics of what you need are easy to identify and collect. The car does not go anywhere without the keys, and directions are essential for reaching the final destination. Similarly, how you plan to achieve the goals of your estate planning can be equally simple, once you know the things that are necessary.

Like taking a road trip to a new place, there are plenty of guidebooks and maps prepared by those who have taken this trip before — ranging from specialized and highly trained professionals to those who have learned from personal experience. Those people can help you do the things that will make your trip unique for you, and there is no need to use up much time and energy figuring it all out on your own. The components of an effective estate plan are all the same; what individualizes each plan is which pieces match your goals and how those components work together.

Although legalese is involved, there are everyday words you can use for the same thing, just like a road that has a state route number (SR 56), a formal name (Lillian Paulsson Memorial Highway), and what the locals call it (Lil's Lane). Sometimes, knowing the description of something is good enough to gain the necessary understanding — e.g., "property is stuff you own" — so that you can still find your way when the map is confusing.

Legally Speaking

A court only recognizes legally binding documents as the way to give your estate to others. Some of these are so widely known and commonly used that descriptions and definitions hardly seem necessary; most people know what a will is and what it is for.

But the difference between what makes a document truly legal, as opposed to what you think is legal, can get you into trouble. If you do not have the right wording, the right number of witnesses, or the right type witnesses, all of your efforts can be ignored.

The following are reoccurring terms you will find throughout this book:

- **Property**: The things you own, which can be anything you want to give to other people; also referred to as principal.

- **Real property**: This is any kind of real estate.

  ▸ *Types*: Vacant land that you buy with the intention of building on, or it might just be an investment that you plan to sell later without developing; your primary residence; a second home, such as a vacation condo; a portion of a home, such as a time-share; investment property, such as a two-family house that you own yourself and which generates rental income; or property in which you share ownership with a partner or business

- Personal property: Your possessions. This category is further divided into tangible personal property — things you can touch — and intangible personal property, or financial assets.

- ▶ *Tangible*: Jewelry, artwork, furniture, china, collectibles such as figurines or antique books, electronic equipment, cars, and boats.
- ▶ *Intangible*: Checking accounts, savings accounts, money market funds, mutual funds, stocks, bonds, or retirement accounts such as a pension, an individual retirement arrangement (IRA), a Roth IRA, or a Keogh plan.

- **Property interest**: This refers to the connection you have to a specific item, piece of land, or other belongings.

  - ▶ *Legal interest*: This is property you can legally transfer or manage but is not yours to use or keep for yourself. Someone who is responsible for the maintenance and oversight of the use of a piece of property but does not legally own it is called a trustee.

    — **Example**: Steve manages the house and grounds of his great-grandmother Julie's family home because she lives in a nursing home. He calls a plumber and contracts to have work done so that the backed-up drains are fixed. Steve might even place an ad in the paper to rent the house, screen applicants, and serve as the primary contract for the renter, collecting rent and addressing problems. However, the property is in Julie's name, and Steve cannot sell the house or any of the land because it belongs to her.

  - ▶ *Beneficial interest*: You receive a benefit from the property.

    — **Example**: Veronica always wanted to go to art school, but she thought the tuition was too expensive, even with student loans. After she graduated from high school, her grandfather told her he had set up a trust fund for her, and the proceeds from that trust will pay her tuition and fees for art school.

- **Ownership**: What the individual or individuals who hold the legal title to a piece of property have. The ability to retain, sell, or give away this property depends on the number of people who hold that title (in some cases, it also depends on their relationship) and any legal agreements/contracts connected to the property.

  ▸ *Sole ownership*: A single person holds the title to the property.

    — **Example**: Mandy owns her car because she paid cash for it, and the title of the car is in her name.

  ▸ *Joint ownership*: When any two people hold an equal share of the title to a piece of property. The most common form is spousal — i.e., when a legally married couple has both names on a title to a piece of property.

    — **Example**: Joe and Mary are listed on the mortgage and the deed to the home they live in together.

- **Community property**: A state law that views a wife and husband as equal partners and assumes a 50/50 split of ownership. New York is not a community property state. There are only nine community property states: Arizona, California, Idaho, Louisiana, Nevada, New Mexico, Texas, Washington, and Wisconsin.

    — **Example**: When Clyde and Bonnie divorced, everything they owned that was not a specific gift from a family member or something owned before or after the marriage was lumped together and divided into two equal parts.

- **Separate property**: Things that are owned by one spouse that are not part of the couple's community property.

— **Example**: Fred owned an antique Model A before he and Carrie married, and the title is in his name.

- **Joint tenancy**: A group of people hold equal and undivided title to a piece of property, which is recognized in New York.

    — **Example**: Brian, Joseph, and Greg own a cottage together in Michigan. All their names are on the deed to the property, and they schedule their vacation time so that everyone has an opportunity to use the cottage.

- **Exemption**: This is a specific amount of money that will not be affected by estate taxes. Federal taxes and states with an estate tax often set an amount, such as $3 million, that is tax-free. Taxes would then be due on $3,000,001 and beyond. New York's tax threshhold for estate tax is currently $1 million.

    ▸ **Donor**: The person who gives a gift or bequest.

    ▸ **Beneficiary**: The individual(s) or group(s) that will receive the property in a will or trust. This can be a single person (a nephew), a group of people (all grandchildren), one group (Stray Cat Rescue, Inc.), several groups (all community councils in your city), or a combination of any of these.

    ▸ **Distribution**: The disbursement or payment of property from an account to a beneficiary. It could be in the form of a check of some other monetary payment, or it could be the transfer of a title into the name of the beneficiary.

You will see many of these terms throughout this book, and some definitions will be expanded upon in sections that provide more detailed information.

Defining Your Estate

Understanding what property is and how ownership is determined makes it possible for you to define your estate. Making a list of what constitutes your estate and what makes up the estate of a spouse or life partner will make it easier to understand some of the choices you have for creating your own plan.

This list, combined with the fundamental values you defined in Chapter 2, will help you consider how a specific estate-planning component might be a good tool for you. There are many choices to make, and it will not be possible to make final decisions quickly, but having some information about your estate in mind while you learn can make the process go more smoothly.

Pass the Parchment

Many important books and legal documents were printed on parchment. Only the wealthy could read, write, or afford to buy parchment for their private use or for special occasions, such as drafting the Declaration of Independence. Even though most of the documents that make up your retirement plan will not have the same historical impact as that document had, it is important to make sure the documentation you do is complete and accurate. If you forget a clause or use the wrong word, the directions you leave will not be worth the paper they are printed on.

What the document is, what it can do, and the laws affecting each will help you choose the elements of your estate plan that will transform your thoughts and wishes into action.

Will

What it is: A legal document in which you identify the people or institutions that should receive money and property from your estate after your death. It also serves to appoint guardianship of children or adults who are your legal responsibility and designate an executor to manage your estate after you die.

What it does:

- It spells out your instructions and wishes for what you want done with the property you leave behind.

- Your affairs go from being private to public when you use a will because it becomes a part of public record — if you want privacy, keep your will basic and legal. *For more information on this, see Chapter 5.*

The laws that matter:

- State laws govern the execution of the instructions in a will. In New York, for example, the surrogate court handles probating of a will according to New York law.

- A will can be challenged and directions contained within it overturned by a judge.

Potential problems:

- Thinking a will is unnecessary or is all you need. Each extreme limits your estate plan's effectiveness.

- Using a will form from the grocery store or the Internet. Unless you understand the laws of New York and how the language of that document matches up, you could have a false sense of security about what will happen after your death. Chapter 11 covers common points about New York wills.

Will substitute

What it is: An agreement, contract, or other legal arrangement that accomplishes the same goals of a will — to protect and transfer property rights — but without the use of a will document. Some options are:

- Holding property in a living trust or joint tenancy.

- Payable-on-death account — the ownership of a monetary account, like a savings account, which is set up to automatically transfer the ownership of the beneficiary upon the death of the donor.

- Financial arrangements that have a named beneficiary — life insurance, IRAs, or pension plans.

What it does:

- These arrangements can save time because the ownership automatically transfers to the beneficiary upon the death of the donor, so it skips the probate process.

- Privacy is preserved, again, because the substitute does not go through probate and is not subject to open-records laws.

- They can also save money because probate court fees are not needed, and some estate taxes can be avoided.

- An unconventional situation — such as multiple ex-spouses and blended families with children from previous marriages — might be better addressed with a will substitute.

The laws that matter:

- Tax laws of New York and the federal government; there is a significant amount of misinformation about what is tax-exempt and what is not.

Potential problems:

- Missing details — each form of will substitute has its own quirks and legal requirements; not having enough signatures, witnesses, or clauses could nullify the entire document. Using the wrong language can also submarine your efforts.

- Find a qualified professional to help you close all the holes in your documents.

Trust

What it is:

A legal arrangement that involves the transfer of property from the original owner to a person or company. The trust holds and maintains the property for the benefit of a specific individual, group of people, or institution(s).

What it does:

The legal arrangement will hold any property in a tax-free account until distributions are made to people or institutions other than the donor, depending on the kind of trust and the beneficiary, or until the entire trust is turned over to a beneficiary.

The laws that matter:

- Taxes, again. Some trusts are tax-exempt; some taxes must be paid by the beneficiary when distributions are made, or the ownership of the trust changes from your name to the beneficiary. Be sure to know what the tax implications are — not all trusts are created equal.

- Exemptions also apply here — trusts for education, a spouse, and for other reasons can eliminate taxes in the distribution or transfer of a trust.

Potential problems:

- Choosing a trust that will not achieve the results you want. Many sales reps will make a commission off the trust you establish, so they might be looking at how to maximize their profit.

- Thinking a trust is all you need.

Insurance

What it is:

A method of protecting valuables in the form of a policy in which premiums are paid over time to guarantee a specific payment for a specific purpose by the company accepting the premiums. Those valuables can be property — home, car, jewelry — a person's life, or the ability to work and care for yourself — life, disability, health care, long-term care.

What it does:

- These various policies protect an estate from the devastation an unexpected accident or terrible illness can bring to your finances. They can preserve your assets and allow you to spend/distribute them as you choose.

- For a small investment, insurance can dramatically increase the value of your estate.

- Some insurance policies only pay a percentage amount — long-term disability might only replace 50 percent of your pre-disability income — so what you receive depends on another factor, like your income.

The laws that matter:

- Taxes, again. Know what insurance income is taxable — disability insurance payments, death benefits, and other kinds of insurance might be subject to local, state, and federal income taxes or estate taxes, depending on the age of the beneficiary.

Potential problems:

- Buying more insurance than you can afford; once you stop paying premiums, the policy will no longer pay benefits.

- Believing that buying insurance is all the estate planning you need to do.

Taxes

What they are:

Estate taxes are fees levied by federal and state governments against property that is left behind after a person dies. Gift taxes are fees levied by federal and state governments against property that is transferred to someone before the owner dies.

What they do:

Taxes affect the amount of money your beneficiaries do or do not receive, because all bills, including taxes, get paid out before your beneficiaries see a dime. Carefully investigate what taxes must be paid on the property you leave behind and who is responsible for paying.

The laws that matter:

- There are all kinds of loopholes that were created and filled over the years, so federal and state tax codes in particular can be extremely confusing. It is impossible to provide a specific list.

- This is where a professional is essential to avoid fines, late fees, and other charges on top of the taxes already owed.

Potential problems:

- Thinking that you will not have to pay any taxes after you die. You might not be around to write the check, but that does not stop the government from sending a bill.

- A failure to leave instructions for your executor about money you set aside specifically for the purpose of paying your estate's taxes could result in the sale of assets or other mistakes in the management of your affairs.

- An executor's failing to file your final income tax and the necessary estate tax forms can have serious consequences for your executor and the bequests you want others to receive.

Retirement funds/pension

What it is:

Money saved in different kinds of accounts with the intention of using those funds to pay for living expenses after a person is no longer employed full-time. There are employer-sponsored accounts — profit-sharing plan, stock bonus plan, employee stock ownership plan (ESOP), and 401(k); individual accounts — IRA, Roth IRA, annuity, variable annuity, or a Keogh plan; and government benefits in the form of social security retirement benefits, Medicare, and disability.

What it does:

- Funds saved for retirement are supposed to make it possible for seniors to live comfortably without working, but planning and the right kind of saving are essential to achieving that goal.

- There are no guarantees: Just because you save does not mean the money will be there. As more companies renege on retirement plans and under-fund employer pension contributions, the retirement you think you will have might not be possible.

The laws that matter:

- There are serious financial penalties imposed on funds removed from retirement accounts before you reach retirement age.

- Social security benefits are taxed as income.

Potential problems:

- Believing that government benefits will be enough to live on when you retire.

- Pension plans that are not insured might not deliver the benefits promised.

In the end, your estate plan might look similar to that of your spouse, or it could be completely different. It all depends on the components you value most and how you handle financial matters. Here is a bumper-sticker summary of how your estate plan might look:

"Fly first class; your kids will, after you are gone."

Ferdie and Lilly, married 65 years with three grown, independent daughters

Will: Separate wills written at the same time, leaving everything to the surviving spouse with specific bequests of heirlooms to family and sentimental tokens to friends, with everything else going to the church in which they were married after both are gone.

Living will: Instructions to not use any extraordinary life-sustaining efforts should they experience a loss of brain function or a disease that impairs their ability to make sound decisions.

Life insurance: One policy was already cashed out to pay for an Alaskan cruise. A second policy will be used to pay for funeral expenses for the first who dies, and the last policy will be used for the survivor.

Pension plan: Spending the dividends every month; whatever is left goes into the travel fund.

Living trust: Spending the dividends every month and using the rest for road trips.

Charitable trust: All property is held in trust for the church and the animal rescue and shelter.

"Yours, Mine, and Mine."

Andrea, divorced with no children and living single for more than 40 years

Will: Does not have one; Andrea lives on a houseboat that she rents, and all her possessions fit into whatever car she leases, so there is nothing to bequest.

Living will: Does not have one.

Life insurance: Three policies — one for Mom, one for Dad, and one for all death-related expenses.

Disability insurance: Short-term, long-term, and extended-care insurance policies.

Retirement accounts: Her 401(k), Roth IRA, and stock bonus plans will cover her monthly expenses, and whatever is left goes into a rainy-day account.

Trust: Her cabin and land she owns on Whidbey Island in Washington, where she plans to retire.

"The one with the most toys wins!"

John Richard Greenman, XIV, and Maya E. Primwater, not married but living together for 18 years, no children — his and hers estate planning

John Richard Greenman, XIV

Will: Fifty percent of everything not in trust goes to Maya; there is just enough information in the will to make it legally binding and uncontestable.

Living will: Instructions on how to use or refrain from using any and all extraordinary life-sustaining efforts.

Life insurance: Multiple policies with multiple beneficiaries, including parents, siblings, long-time family servants, and a few elderly female relatives.

Retirement accounts: All set to roll over into trust funds to support the educational efforts of all subsequent generations of nieces and nephews, contingent upon achieving specific grade point averages, with financial rewards for exceeding those levels.

Living trust: Spending the dividends every month on lavish parties, resort vacations, and redoing the summer house in the Hamptons.

Charitable remainder trust: Several specific charities get the "leftovers," which will be approximately $11 million.

Social security: Benefits will go to support arts organizations.

Maya E. Primwater

Will: 50 percent of everything not in trust goes to "Johnny," with just enough information in the will to make it legally binding and uncontestable.

Living will: Instructions to use or not use extraordinary life-sustaining efforts or do-not-resuscitate orders.

Life insurance: Multiple policies with multiple beneficiaries including siblings, lifelong friends, and charities.

Retirement accounts: All set to roll over into an endowment fund to provide ongoing support for more than two dozen charities and non-profits for which Maya volunteers.

Living trust: Spending the dividends every month on visits to overseas non-profit organizations doing research for her endowment.

Education trust funds: Several funds are set up to send her nieces and nephews, cousins, and the children of close friends to study abroad; other funds are set up for "self-study" for those who want to find their way in a less academic environment.

Social security: Benefits will go to support local social justice groups.

Whatever money is left in her retirement accounts is to be placed in trust after her death to establish a writers' retreat that will be operated by the Write on the Sound Writer's Conference.

By looking over these hypothetical estate plans, you can begin to see how the things you value might impact the decisions you make.

• *Did You Know?* •

The person who will eventually administer your estate has some basic guidelines to follow due to state and federal laws regarding this task. Specific taxes must be paid by certain deadlines. An extension can be granted, but only if the paperwork is completed in a certain way, submitted to the correct office, and signed by a specific person or judge. You can help make this process flow a little more smoothly by keeping that in mind and planning for some potential problems.

☑ Watch Out for This!

☐ Prepare a letter with details about how to administer your estate.

☐ Provide as much detailed information as possible about your estate. Annual updates to your documents will mean fewer undocumented items for the executor to track down.

☐ Bonding requirements for your executor can be waived if you include language in your will to that effect. If your executor is a bank, you might want to keep those in place, but for a family member, this might not be necessary.

☐ Death or probate notices must be filed as part of estate proceedings; you can assist your executor with a list of addresses of pertinent parties for your estate.

Your executor should be aware of the following items:

☐ Publish the death notices properly to avoid disputes.

☐ Be diligent in identifying and inventorying assets; an apparent lack of effort can result in legal trouble.

☐ Ask questions about anything that is unclear in legal documents and estate administration instructions, and get clarification in writing. This can help avoid potential disputes or help address those that do arise.

Details neither of you control:

☐ Disputes raised by creditors or dissatisfaction about how a claim is settled.

☐ Disagreements between and challenges brought by beneficiaries.

☐ Claims made by a spouse against an estate that conflict with the terms of a will; some states, including New York, entitle a spouse to a specific percentage of an estate regardless of the decedent's wishes.

CASE STUDY: COMPONENTS OF AN EFFECTIVE ESTATE PLAN

Anne Marie Griffith
Tom Kotick
SS&G Financial Services, Inc.
Certified Public Accountants and
Advisers
tkotick@ssandg.com

What is essential to include in an estate plan?

Estate planning is the process of developing and implementing a master plan that facilitates the distribution of your property after your death according to your goals and objectives.

The critical pieces involved in estate planning involve the following documents: a will; a trust in the case of minor children, a large estate, or second marriage with children from prior marriages; durable powers of attorney; a living will and a medical power of attorney or medical proxy; and a letter of instructions is also recommended. Other critical priorities of the estate-planning process involve the selection of an executor/executrix for your will/estate, a guardian for your minor children, and trustees or co-trustees in the case of any trusts created. Finally, a cash-flow analysis and some income-tax planning should be part of the priority list for the estate-planning playbook.

Anyone with property or minor children should have a will. While most people think of the will as the driving factor determining where your property goes, beneficiary designations and the titling of assets often play a bigger role in this determination. For example, when someone owns property as joint tenants with rights of survivorship, this property will go to the joint owner, regardless of what a will says. Also, many assets are governed by beneficiary designations, such as retirement plans and life insurance. These types of assets will always pass by way of the beneficiary designation, not according to a person's will.

Life insurance is one of the biggest players in the estate-planning game. For some, it is the only way to ensure that family members will be able to support themselves after the death of the primary wage earner. For those with larger estates, life insurance can provide the funds needed to pay estate taxes (and other costs) without liquidating estate assets. For those with a business interest, life insurance can be used as a vehicle for business succession. Finally, for those with a generous spirit, life insurance can permit you to make charitable gifts.

What are the most common mistakes people make? What do people forget to include?

A very common mistake is not addressing the estate-planning process at all, which can result in what is called "dying intestate," or dying without a will. In that case, the distribution of the estate and the care of minor children are resolved by the state.

Another oversight is not funding the estate to properly care for your spouse or your minor or school-aged children in terms of ongoing financial needs for daily living and future educational costs.

Other common mistakes or oversights are in the need for annual income-tax filings for any trusts that have been created, or gift-tax return filings in the case of gifts over the annual exclusion amount.

What are the benefits of working with someone in your field?

A CPA who is experienced in working with clients on their personal financial plans, which include estate planning, can help avoid the mistakes and oversights mentioned previously.

The CPA can effectuate the "quarterbacking" of the estate-planning process. This is done in several ways, including assisting the attorney in drafting the documents in accordance with the client's needs and desires, as well as recommending a good estate attorney if the client does not enter the process with an attorney; coordinating the work of the investment/broker to properly identify and re-title assets; and working with the life insurance agent to make sure ongoing living and educational expenses are covered with the right amount and type of life insurance coverage and policy.

The CPA is usually involved in the preparation of any annual trust or gift-tax filing requirements that might spring from the planning process. The CPA will gather the information necessary to make the filings by coordinating the assistance and necessary input from the other team members to make the proper filings each year.

How does a person go about choosing a professional in your field?

If a client is working with a CPA for his annual personal and/or business accounting and tax work, you can start by asking if she does estate planning as well as income taxes. Or you can ask your CPA for a referral to a CPA who is experienced in the financial-planning process involving estate planning.

It helps qualify the CPA if he/she has certain additional certifications, such as the PFS (Personal Financial Specialist) designation, or a CFP® (Certified Financial Planner®). Also helpful is a CPA who has studied for and retains a state life-insurance license.

CHAPTER 4

Taxes

When Roman Emperor Caesar Augustus was running short on cash to pay for things like aqueducts and parties, he created the first estate levy. Ever since then, death and taxes have been linked. Unfortunately, our version of that original tax law has become complicated and confusing over time.

When one loophole is discovered, a new rule is created to cover it. But then that rule has a little wiggle room that needs to be closed up, so another rule is created — and the cycle continues. So do not count on an easy answer to the question of how much tax money your estate will have to pay after you die. Your best bet is to track down people who specialize in tax law — a CPA or an attorney.

The gross estate, which is the value of all property owned by the deceased person on the date of death, is what gets taxed. The federal government gets a chunk based on the Estate Recovery Act — the estate tax, referred to as the "death tax" by those in Congress who want to completely do away with it. There are some states that have a state estate tax similar to that of the federal government, though other states levy a tax on the property received by the beneficiary — an inheritance tax. New York has an estate tax dependent on the federal tax scheme. It does not impose an inheritance tax. All these taxes have a host of exemptions or deductions that reduce or eliminate the taxes that need to be paid.

Strategically using the exemptions and deductions and also creating tax-free accounts makes it possible to get around some of these taxes. That is one of the best benefits of estate planning. Before you can save taxes, you need to know what they are and how much you might owe. Without a crystal ball or clairvoyance, it is impossible to know what the precise worth of your estate will be at the time of your death, but planning for what you do know puts you in a position to help your loved ones avoid some painful tax bills.

Keep in mind that no matter how much you prepare, the tax laws can be changed with the stroke of a pen in Washington, D.C., or Albany, and everything you thought you knew and planned for can be changed. Consider all the information in this section to be accompanied by an asterisk, which means subject to change at any time; do not consider this information to be the definitive legal authority.

Check with a tax professional who is current with federal and state-tax law changes.

Federal First

There are three federal taxes that directly affect your estate: the gift tax, the generation-skipping transfer tax, and the estate tax.

Any gift you give to another person or institution — in cash or the transfer of property — in one fiscal year is subject to a gift tax. There is one exemption: The first $13,000 given to any single person or organization is exempt from the tax, but everything from $13,001 and beyond is subject to taxation.

Example: You decide to give your niece Meghan $5,000 as a high school graduation present because she wants to tour Europe before going to college.

Do you owe? No. Because this gift is under $13,000, you do not owe any taxes on this gift.

But...

You can only give Meghan another $8,000 this year and have it be tax-free. If you make the next gift $9,000, you will owe the gift tax on $1,000.

As the donor, the person who gives a gift, you are eligible for some tax deductions that might also make the tax bill go away. The donee, the person or institution receiving the gift, is what determines the deduction or exclusion you can apply:

Tax deductions — your spouse, many charities
Exclusions — medical expenses, political organizations, tuition

Example: Your husband has an opportunity to buy a workshop full of woodworking tools from an elderly neighbor who is giving up the hobby. He has his own checking account, but it was his turn to add money to the kids' college fund this month and he does not have enough cash. So, you give him the money from your checking account.

Do you owe? No. The marital tax deduction means you can give your spouse $150,000 in a year and it is tax-free.

But...

If you try to do the same thing with the man you have lived with for 18 years and are not married to, you will have to pay the gift tax on $137,000. You still get to take advantage of the annual $13,000 exemption.

Like most things, these deductions and exclusions all have fine print. To have an unlimited, tax-free marital deduction, your spouse must be married and a U.S. citizen at the time the gift is made.

Example: It is Friday night, and your grandson Thomas calls, absolutely frantic. His tuition is due the following week, and he cannot reach Mom (she is out of state at a convention). Dad has not been around for years — and even if he were, he almost certainly would not have the $13,200 he owes. You write down the name of the school, address, and all of the particulars so that you can have your bank transfer the funds on Monday.

Do you owe? No. For the education exclusion to be on the up-and-up, the gift must be paid directly to the educational institution, so you will not owe any taxes.

But…

The education exclusion is for tuition or training only. Thomas is on his own for books, unless you give him additional cash.

When it comes to charities, they must be qualified by the Internal Revenue Service (IRS). You cannot just give money to an animal shelter and deduct that from your taxes; you have to make sure the IRS has decided it is a charity, and the gifts you give to a charity need to fit into predetermined categories:

- **Outright charitable gift:** This is property that you give to a charity without getting anything in return. The gift can be cash or any other type of property.

- **Bargain sale**: The sale of a piece of property to a charity at a rate that is below the fair market value. The difference between the amount paid and the actual value is the amount of the gift.

- **Stock bailout:** The transfer of stock ownership from your name to that of the charity. The fair market value of the stock at the time of the transfer is the gift amount.

There are many other conditions that must be met to make your gift tax-free, regardless of who gets the gift. That is why you must consult with a tax expert to make sure your interpretation of your gift matches what the government allows. Unless you are a whiz at tax law, you are in all probability going to need some help navigating the ever-changing federal estate tax.

In 2001, a law called the Economic Growth and Tax Relief Reconciliation Act was passed that increased the exemption for the estate tax. In 2002 and 2003, taxes were owed on anything over $1 million. So, if your estate was worth $1.5 million, you only had to pay tax on $500,000. At a 45 percent tax rate — the highest federal tax rate for an estate — the exemptions create a limit to the money the feds can collect. The exemption increased to $3.5 million until 2009, then the tax was repealed in 2010 until 2011, when the exemption goes back down to $1 million — unless Congress steps in and repeals the tax for good.

For a while, some people managed to dodge the estate tax dilemma. A person with a multi-million-dollar estate did not want to have less money to give to her beneficiaries, so she named her grandchildren or great-grandchildren as the beneficiaries. They are all minors, so they do not have to pay any taxes on their inheritance. However, the federal government caught on to that and created a tax specifically designed to tax the money skipping over generations. Called the Generation-Skipping Tax Transfer (GSTT), it is the most complex tax law, according to the experts in the field.

There are entire books written about this topic, and they still do not encompass all the details. Suffice it to say, if your estate is worth more than $2 million, you will want to work with an estate-tax planner to make sure you look at the implications of trying to give all your worldly goods to the youngest of your family tree.

• *Did You Know?* •

Children under the age of 14 are required to pay income tax at the single-person tax rate on income earned through employment. They must file a tax return like everyone else, but they get special treatment by the IRS if their parents are wealthy and try to give a large sum of money.

"Kiddie tax" is the term used to describe income tax applied to money that minors did not earn through employment, also called unearned income. In 1996, a special law was created to close a loophole that allowed parents to give their children a large gift as a way to pay a lower tax on the interest earned. The child tax rate was significantly lower than the adult rate.

The law has changed over the years, and in 2008 it changed again. The first $900 in income made on any investment in a child's name — age 19 and younger, extending to the age of 24 if the child is in school full-time — is not subject to income tax. The next $900 is subject to a 10 percent tax, up to $90. Anything above $1,800 is taxed at the tax rate of the child's parent(s).

☑Watch Out for This!

☐ You can take advantage of your child's lower income-tax bracket by investing in U.S. Savings Bonds. The income is deferred, and so are the taxes.

☐ Money paid to your child in the form of wages for working in your business is not subject to the "kiddie tax." Those payments are deductible by your business, but it is important to keep the necessary records for hours and work performed. Not having these could make it appear as though you are trying to cheat on your business taxes.

☐ A child earning her own income and paying taxes can still be declared as a dependent on a parent's tax return, allowing that parent to take a standard deduction. If you divorce and do not get custody of the children, you do not get "custody" of the standard deduction for your taxes.

Now for the State

Most states hold out for some of your estate as well. Some, like New York, levy an estate tax similar to or related to the federal law, which means your estate may owe taxes on the property you leave behind, according to its net value. Because these taxes are tied to the federal tax, you need to make sure you are looking at the most current, correct federal estate-tax tables — and the most current state of the law, which is subject to change — to know what the New York estate tax will be.

Other states levy a tax on the property received by a beneficiary — an inheritance tax. As mentioned, New York does not. In the states that do, generally the closer the relationship the beneficiary has to the deceased, the lower his tax will be. For example, a brother will have a larger exemption and will therefore have a lower tax rate than a distant cousin.

Some states also impose a state gift tax. New York had one, but it repealed its gift tax as of January 1, 2000. To find out whether your state has such a tax, whether there is an annual exclusion, lifetime exemptions for close family members, or for any other legal technicalities, a good place to begin is the state's department of revenue or taxation.

Another one is the state income tax. Tax on income earned during a fiscal year may be levied on residents of the state. You can be a full- or part-time resident, or simply live in the state for a few months out of the year. Income earned in another state might be taxable in New York.

Mistakes Happen... Frequently

The only federal regulation that might be more complex than tax law is immigration law. This complexity means people make costly mistakes, miss savings opportunities, and wind up confused about what can and cannot be done legally. Most tax specialists are CPAs or lawyers, and it is their job to stay ahead of the latest changes to the ever-growing tax code.

Over time, some common mistakes related to taxes and estate planning have emerged. This list is a sample of those errors; they can help you identify holes in your own planning, help you prepare for a meeting with a tax advisor, and, at the very least, inspire you not to get careless about managing this element of your own estate plan.

Mistakes your executor can make include:.02

- Using the wrong IRS forms when filing taxes. This can involve consulting the wrong tables and filling out and submitting the wrong schedule — like using the 1040 EZ income tax form when, by law, you are required to use the 1040 long form.

- Missing information about your estate. If you do not provide or disclose all the information, your executor might not know about an account that is taxable, making him or her liable for any oversight that occurs. The "But he didn't tell me" defense will not work.

- Not having the necessary record to justify or back up the filing. This can mean having no mileage record, and missing receipts and account interest statements.

- Preparing a return without professional help. Professionals who are up-to-date on all the current tax laws can help an executor avoid a multitude of mistakes, such as using the wrong form or having insufficient documentation

- Miscalculations. This can involve transposing numbers or just coming up with the wrong number when adding or subtracting.

- Not signing the tax form. Decision-making mistakes you can make while preparing
an estate plan:

- When to bequeath a gift: before or after death
- How to use gifts that fall below the annual gift-tax exclusion amount ($13,000 for 2010)
- The most advantageous way to structure a life insurance policy
- Selecting a trust with the maximum tax advantages for you and the beneficiary
- When it is best to leave property to a spouse
- Whether to make a bequest that will negatively impact the tax position of the beneficiary.

If you want to look up a specific topic or try your hand at sorting the rules related to a specific estate planning element — such as trusts — refer to **www.irs.gov**.

When, Not If, You Pay

The No. 1 benefit many professionals cite for estate planning is dramatically reducing the estate's tax burden. To effectively do this requires attention to the tax laws of New York and any other state in which you own property.

There are some helpful details to know about taxes when doing your estate planning:

The federal estate tax rate begins at 45 percent and goes as high as 50 percent. It is best to check where those rates stand periodically and every time you review or change your estate plan, to assess the impact on the after-tax value of your estate. Your lawyer is the best person to draft appropriate language for your estate to cover taxes that may be assessed.

Your executor will ultimately have to handle all these money matters. In addition to calculating the value of your estate, she must file a tax return for your estate, called the fiduciary return, with the IRS and make the necessary payments, if there are any. Also, an estate tax and other tax obligations come with a deadline — they cannot just be paid whenever your executor gets around to it. The estate requires some liquidity for covering taxes if they are owed.

If your estate is worth less than $1 million, at the moment, you will not have to worry about federal estate tax, but you might still be looking at state estate taxes, depending on the state. The best way to avoid taxes is to leave your entire estate to your spouse, a charity, or some combination thereof.

Your executor has a few options for saving some tax money, but this is where advice from an estate professional is crucial. If your executor does the wrong thing, it will cost him personally. Your executor should consider the following:

- Be sure all possible deductions are included in the fiduciary return; these include funeral expenses, expenses to your estate (e.g., appraisal fees or probate court costs), debts (e.g., mortgage or credit cards), charitable contributions, and marital deductions. The marital deduction can only be taken if your spouse is a U.S. citizen.

- Value the assets of the estate at a later date as opposed to right at death. This can only be done under the correct circumstances, and whether it is a beneficial move depends upon the individual estate and time of death.

- Income going into the estate can be timed to the advantage of the estate. Timing the sale of property or sending out requests for payments due can be scheduled to the advantage of filing the deceased's last income tax return and the fiduciary return the executor must file for the estate.

- Estate distributions to beneficiaries can also be timed so that the beneficiary must pay the tax, not the estate: If the payments to beneficiaries are made before the fiduciary return is filed, then the estate's value drops, making the taxes due also drop.

Your beneficiaries can also reduce their tax bills (if any) by declining to accept a bequest. Federal and state tax laws permit a disclaimer, which is a refusal to accept a gift. Whether this is a single or joint bequest, one or both parties can decline, but it must be refused in writing, commonly within nine months of your death. This is one of the details your estate-planning specialist should cover with you as necessary.

There are choices you can make in your estate planning before others need to make decisions about how to handle the taxes on your estate. When properly coordinated, some choices create an opportunity to reduce the potential tax burden on your estate and beneficiaries. These are some ways to reduce taxes, so it is a good idea to keep these in the back of your mind while working on your complete estate plan:

- Make gifts before you die to reduce your estate's value.

- Put property into tax-free trusts. See Chapter 6 for more information about your choices.

- Schedule property transfers to take place at the time of your death.

- Coordinate your estate planning with your spouse and divvy up assets to the best advantage for both of you.

- Use permissible exemptions, such as leaving your entire estate to your spouse.

- Consider investing in life insurance and structuring the policies carefully. See Chapter 7 for more information on how this works.

However, like all estate-planning decisions, choosing the wrong options or not using the right language can lay waste to all your careful planning. Do not try this on your own.

• *Did You Know?* •

The fees paid to an executor as compensation for the time she puts into managing and closing out your estate are taxable income. If your executor opts not to accept a fee, then the money you designate for that purpose becomes part of your estate. If it is not held in a tax-free account, that money can be subject to estate tax.

☑ Watch Out for This

☐ Talk to your executor about a fee. If he does not want to be compensated, then you can plan accordingly.

CASE STUDY: TAX ADVICE FROM THE IRS

Internal Revenue Service (IRS)
1-800-829-1040
Hours of Operation: Monday - Friday,
7 a.m. - 10 p.m. your local time
(Alaska & Hawaii follow Pacific Time)
www.irs.gov

The IRS is the ultimate source for all things related to taxation. Its Web site offers extensive resources for those who wish to learn more about anything related to taxes. What follows is a copy of the frequently asked questions (FAQ) on the Estate Taxes page. The IRS is not in the habit of helping people figure out how to reduce their tax bills, but they will give you all you need to know to be "legal." Simply achieving the goal of compliance with tax law is not something even the FAQ can guarantee. The recurring qualifiers and other sources you need to check make it clear that dealing with estate taxes on your own is risky.

When can I expect the Estate Tax Closing Letter?

There can be some variation, but for returns that are accepted as filed and contain no other errors or special circumstances, you should expect to wait about four to six months after the return is filed to receive your closing letter. Returns that are selected for examination or reviewed for statistical purposes will take longer.

What is included in the estate?

The gross estate of the decedent consists of an accounting of everything you own or have certain interests in at the date of death. The fair market value of these items is used, not necessarily what you paid for them or what their values were when you acquired them. The total of all of these items is your gross estate. The includible property may consist of cash and securities, real estate, insurance, trusts, annuities, business interests, and other assets. Keep in mind that the gross estate will likely include non-probate as well as probate property.

I own a ½ interest in a farm (or building or business) with my brother (sister, friend, other). What is included?

Depending on how your ½ interest is held and treated under state law — and how it was acquired — you would probably only include ½ of its value in your gross estate. However, many other factors influence this answer, so you would need to visit with a tax or legal professional to make that determination.

What is excluded from the estate?

Generally, the gross estate does not include property owned solely by the decedent's spouse or other individuals. Lifetime gifts that are complete (no powers or other control over the gifts are retained) are not included in the gross estate (but taxable gifts are used in the computation of the estate tax). Life estates given to the decedent by others in which the decedent has no further control or power at the date of death are not included.

What deductions are available to reduce the estate tax?

1. Marital deduction: One of the primary deductions for married decedents is the marital deduction. All property that is included in the gross estate and passes to the surviving spouse is eligible for the marital deduction. The property must pass "outright." In some cases, certain life estates also qualify for the marital deduction.
2. Charitable deduction: If the decedent leaves property to a qualifying charity, it is deductible from the gross estate.
3. Mortgages and debt.
4. Administration expenses of the estate.
5. Losses during estate administration.

What other information do I need to include with the return?

Among other items listed:

1. Copies of the death certificate
2. Copies of the decedent's will and/or relevant trusts
3. Copies of appraisals
4. Copies of relevant documents regarding litigation involving the estate
5. Documentation of any unusual items shown on the return (partially included assets, losses, near-date-of-death transfers, others)

What is "fair market value?"

Fair market value is defined as "the price at which the property would change hands between a willing buyer and a willing seller, neither being under any compulsion to buy or to sell, and both having reasonable knowledge of relevant facts. The fair market value of a particular item of property includible in the decedent's gross estate is not to be determined by a forced sale price. Nor is the fair market value of an item of property to be determined by the sale price of the item in a market other than that in which such item is most commonly sold to the public, taking into account the location of the item wherever appropriate."

What about the value of my family business/farm?

Generally, the fair market value of such interests owned by the decedent are includible in the gross estate at date of death. However, for certain farms or businesses operated as a family farm or business, reductions to these amounts may be available.

In the case of a qualifying family farm, IRC §2032A allows a reduction from value of up to $820,000.

If the decedent owned an interest in a qualifying family-owned business, a deduction from the gross estate in the amount of up to $1,100,000 may be available under IRC §2057.

What if I do not have everything ready for filing by the due date?

The estate's representative may request an extension of time to file for up to six months from the due date of the return. However, the correct amount of tax is still due by the due date, and interest is accrued on any amounts still owed by the due date that are not paid at that time.

Whom should I hire to represent me and prepare and file the return?

The IRS cannot make recommendations about specific individuals, but there are several factors to consider:

1. How complex is the estate? By the time most estates reach $1,000,000, there is usually some complexity involved.
2. How large is the estate?
3. In what condition are the decedent's records?
4. How many beneficiaries are there, and are they cooperative?
5. Do I need an attorney, CPA, enrolled agent (EA), or other professional(s)?

With these questions in mind, it is a good idea to discuss the matter with several attorneys and CPAs or EAs. Ask about how much experience they have had, and ask for referrals. This process should be similar to locating a good physician. Locate other individuals that have had similar experiences and ask for recommendations. Finally, after the individual(s) are employed and begin to work on estate matters, make sure the lines of communication remain open so that there are no surprises during administration or if the estate tax return is examined.

Finally, most estates engage the services of both attorneys and CPAs or EAs. The attorney usually handles probate matters and reviews the impact of documents on the estate tax return. The CPA or EA often handles the actual return preparation and some representation of the estate in matters with the IRS. However, some attorneys handle all the work. CPAs and EAs may also handle most of the work, but cannot take care of probate matters and other situations where a law license is required. In addition, other professionals (such as appraisers, surveyors, financial advisors and others) may need to be engaged during this time.

Do I have to talk to the IRS during an examination?

You do not have to be present during an examination unless an IRS representative needs to ask specific questions. Although you may represent yourself during an examination, most executors prefer that professional(s) they have employed handle this phase of administration. They may delegate authority for this by signing a designation on the Form 706 itself, or executing Form 2848, "Power of Attorney."

What if I disagree with the examination proposals?

You have many rights and avenues of appeal if you disagree with any proposals made by the IRS.

What happens if I sell property that I have inherited?

The sale of such property is usually considered the sale of a capital asset and may be subject to capital gains (or loss) treatment. However, IRC §1014 provides that the basis of property acquired from a decedent is its fair market value at the date of death, so there is usually little or no gain to account for if the sale occurs soon after the date of death. Remember, the rules are different for determining the basis of property received as a lifetime gift.

Death is Big Business

The federal government is the first beneficiary to get a share of your estate, or any estate in the union. The IRS creates numerous statistics for everything they do, including tracking the number of deaths by state, the number of estates that pay taxes, and the amount of taxes paid. Part of that information is listed below to give you a sense of just how much money was added to the coffers of the U.S. government.

These numbers are in the thousands of dollars. After you add the zeros, you might find a new source of motivation for doing your planning now so your family does not have to pay later.

Statistic of income (SOI) estate tax data tables, Selected years of death

The data included in these SOI tables are for returns filed for decedents who died in the same year and whose estates would have been subject to the same tax law and similar economic conditions.

Estate tax returns filed for 2004 decedents, by state of residence

[All figures are estimates based on a sample — money amounts are in thousands of dollars.]

State of residence	Gross estate, tax purposes [1]		Net estate tax	
Total	42,239	185,921,379	19,294	22,219,722
Alabama	409	1,582,888	186	192,473
Alaska	31	99,483	* 4	* 3,739
Arizona	621	2,408,320	302	311,565
Arkansas	265	974,431	108	117,256
California	8,464	34,208,317	3,782	4,131,248
Colorado	529	1,630,180	232	143,801
Connecticut	783	3,884,353	341	598,826
Delaware	223	721,092	136	87,531
District of Columbia	177	838,357	95	83,900

State of residence	Gross estate, tax purposes [1]		Net estate tax	
Georgia	900	4,077,616	322	405,561
Florida	4,090	20,245,897	1,871	2,635,096
Hawaii	164	677,400	64	61,901
Idaho	109	523,850	40	50,694
Illinois	1,957	8,149,220	999	946,912
Indiana	650	2,831,953	311	317,585
Iowa	474	1,425,778	184	158,665
Kansas	460	1,363,923	178	103,960
Kentucky	329	1,130,537	142	146,137
Louisiana	347	2,018,730	151	147,549
Maine	168	659,868	75	91,739
Maryland	1,065	4,307,335	550	482,638
Massachusetts	1,351	5,074,541	687	604,858
Michigan	951	8,439,720	380	1,217,440
Minnesota	575	2,875,632	203	489,367
Mississippi	188	803,735	97	126,962
Missouri	809	3,273,612	379	431,486
Montana	142	387,347	59	20,450
Nebraska	292	3,864,505	153	238,470
Nevada	300	1,523,564	164	211,414
New Hampshire	207	682,735	102	94,771
New Jersey	1,528	5,845,773	719	583,693
New Mexico	200	581,845	96	68,503
New York	3,156	17,657,621	1,539	2,425,496
North Carolina	970	3,709,205	430	409,190
North Dakota	45	233,142	* 18	* 12,693
Ohio	1,360	5,276,026	552	457,293
Oklahoma	320	1,146,682	173	147,687
Oregon	306	1,271,623	156	117,853
Pennsylvania	1,497	6,044,429	641	618,191
Rhode Island	197	675,120	69	69,145
South Carolina	285	1,429,461	131	126,410
South Dakota	113	559,505	* 21	* 8,229
Tennessee	519	1,907,851	228	206,705
Texas	1,708	7,601,993	833	1,021,141
Utah	136	582,465	43	68,946

State of residence	Gross estate, tax purposes [1]		Net estate tax	
Vermont	94	606,845	33	87,589
Virginia	1,149	4,106,031	507	470,479
Washington	720	2,527,374	294	275,636
West Virginia	171	485,637	106	53,936
Wisconsin	592	2,332,999	309	248,192
Wyoming	62	220,794	41	23,807
Other areas [2]	81	434,037	58	64,917

NOTE: Detail may not add to total because of rounding.

* Estimates should be used with caution because of the small number of sample returns on which they were based.

[1] Gross estate is shown at the value used to determine estate tax liability. The value could be determined as of the decedent's date of death or six months thereafter (i.e., alternate valuation method).

[2] Includes U.S. territories, U.S. citizens domiciled abroad, and a small number of returns for whom state of residence was unknown.

CHAPTER 5

Wills

A family, dressed head to toe in black, sitting around Grandpa's book-lined study, fidgets while the elderly lawyer sitting behind the leather-topped desk cleans his glasses and clears his throat before rasping, "Being of sound mind and body…" The scene is pure Hollywood, but most lawyers will tell you to save the drama for personal letters and keep your will legally correct to avoid potential problems. Make sure beneficiaries know what they are getting so that the day after the funeral, your family can be at home and not in a lawyer's office getting tied up in more drama.

A will is a legal document in which you identify what people or institutions receive money and property from your estate after your death. It also serves to appoint guardianship of children or adults who are your legal responsibility and designates, as well as an executor to manage your estate after you die. With standard will forms available on the Internet, it would seem that preparing a will is easy. But choosing the wrong kind of will, not having enough witnesses, leaving out key language required by New York, or having inadequate particulars can mean the state, not you, will decide what happens to your estate.

There are things called will substitutes, such as a living trust, that can accomplish many of the things a will is designed to do, but it is still a good idea to have a will in addition to your other estate-planning options. That is because the state imposes a will on you if you do not write one of your own. If you die leaving possessions behind, someone has to divvy them up — and the state assumes that responsibility if you do not do a good job of it.

When you die, if you have a valid will, you die "testate." If you do not have a will when you die, then you are "intestate," and there are laws in New York that determine what happens to your belongings. The legal system will distribute your assets, not you. Because your debts have to be paid when you die, including federal and state taxes, your creditors get paid first, then your beneficiaries will get what is left over.

Most experts will tell you that, for the relatively low cost of having a will prepared by a lawyer, the safety and protection it provides is worth the investment of time and money. But before you can ask about one, you need to know what goes into a will.

Will Basics

To make sure your will is legal and can be executed, some essential information is necessary. Using your legal name in your will — the one that is on your birth certificate and under which you file your tax returns — makes it harder for someone to challenge your will, be that the state, a person, or an institution.

The address listed in your will should be the state in which you vote, hold a driver's license, and have your primary residence. Documentation is necessary to prove the state in which you live. As previously mentioned, if you are a resident of New York, the surrogate court will have jurisdiction over your will.

Another important point about where you live is whether your state has a community property law on the books. If so, then whatever property falls into your state's definition of community property will be jointly owned by a wife and a husband, potentially limiting what you can do with that property in your will. Remember, though, that New York is not a community property state.

Another state-related issue is ownership of property outside New York. If you live in New York but own a condominium in another state, the out-of-state property will not be handled by the New York court. The court in the state where the property is located will oversee the transition of ownership. When preparing your will, you need to take this into account. Just because you own it does not mean you get to control what happens to it after your death.

Wills Defined

The will that most people think of, called a simple will, is a legal document that applies to only one person. However, all wills, to be legal, need to include a number of elements. The will needs to identify who you are, your beneficiaries, your executor, the directions you leave for the care of people for whom you are responsible, and the distribution of your assets.

These are basic elements every will needs to have:

- **Beneficiary**: The individual(s) or group(s) that will receive the property.

- **Executor**: Also called a personal representative, this is the individual who handles the property you are leaving behind. If you die without a will, the court appoints an administrator, frequently a spouse or adult child, who will serve in the same capacity of handling all the paperwork, preparing of assets, dealing with likely heirs, handling claims from creditors, making payments on outstanding debt, and other estate-related matters.

- **Clauses**: The sections in your will that likely organize the information in a specific order.

  ▸ **Opening clauses**: Lay out the basic information about who you are and set the stage for the clauses that follow:

    — *Introductory clause* identifies you as the person who is making the will.

    — *Family-statement clause* introduces and identifies the family members who will be referred to later in the will.

    — *Tax clause* explains how the taxes of your estate will be paid.

  ▸ **Survival clause**: This leaves everything in your estate to one named person. Married people frequently do this to ensure that everything goes to the surviving spouse.

  ▸ **Guardianship clause**: The appointment of a guardian for minor children (under the age of 21 in New York); a successor guardian should also be named as a backup. In New York, you can appoint a standby guardian during your lifetime.

  ▸ **Giving clauses**: These clauses leave specific bequests, or property that is identified by name and description, to beneficiaries and explain what property goes to which person and under what circumstances. These can be as broad or explicit as you want. They are divided up according to the following categories:

    — *Real property clauses:* Statements that match up property with a person. For example: You want your spouse, Susan, to have the house, and your brother, Fred, to have your antique baseball card collection.

    — *Personal property clauses:* Used when you want to be explicit in your instructions. For example: You want Teddy to get the Google stock, and Elizabeth gets the General Motors stock.

▶ **Residuary clause, or residue**: Addresses the "leftovers," the balance of your estate that you do not single out in detail in a specific clause. The residuary clause is essential for any kind of will to make sure that anything you forget or might have acquired after the will was prepared can be distributed. Naming at least one beneficiary is a good idea to keep your assets out of the hands of the courts; naming two or more alternative beneficiaries is better. For example: You want Bertha Jones, your second cousin twice removed, and her husband, Bubba Jones, to benefit from what is not given to anyone else. If either or both of them predeceases you, then all of the balance of your estate goes to Bubba Jones, Jr.

▶ **Appointment clause**: Identifies the person who will manage your estate. For example, suppose Robert Anthony, your best friend since college, will serve as the executor of your estate.

▶ **Fiduciary powers clause**: The language that gives your executor the power to serve as your executor, including any duties that go beyond the basic requirements in New York. For example, suppose Robert Anthony will have the ability to provide your spouse, children, and parents with income until your estate is settled.

▶ **Ending clauses**: These include the legalities to meet statutory requirements so that your will is legal and valid, which include (but are not limited to) your signature, date, location of the signing, and witnesses.

Your will can be as broad or specific as you choose. As one piece of your overall estate plan, your will should be seen as one of several tools and prepared accordingly.

If you want to keep your affairs private, then a more broad will would be in order. Once a will is entered in court, anyone can read it because it becomes a public record. If you have seen the children of a deceased friend get into fistfights over a raggedy old couch or go to court over an off-shore investment account, you might want to go into more detail.

There are different kinds of wills from which to choose to meet your specific needs. The format of these wills changes depending on who is represented in the will, what the will is designed to do, or how it is prepared.

Tips for Creating Your Will

Essentials elements for a valid will include:

- **Being in written form.** Wills that are given orally might not stand up in court. New York does recognize oral (nuncupative) wills in limited circumstances.
- **Your name and age.**
- **"Being of sound mind."** This means you know the property in your possession and the people or institutions identified as beneficiaries.
- **Clear statement and intention to transfer property.**
- **Signed voluntarily.**
- **Witnessed properly.**
- **Executed properly.** The will must include a statement that attests to the fact that this is your will, the date, the place it is signed, and that it is signed in front of witnesses.

A few more things...

The original document

If the original will is stored in a safe deposit box, it could become inaccessible after your death if that box is in your name only. Have your lawyer or executor retain the original will in his or her files so that it is readily accessible. Other will-related documents

Your original durable power of attorney, medical power of attorney, living will, and any other documents related to incapacitation should also be stored in your lawyer's office or other trusted representative. Those taking responsibility for making medical, financial, or other decisions ought to have a copy of that power of attorney.

> **Copies**
>
> Choosing to keep your will private is a decision you will need to make based on a conversation with your lawyer. Unusual clauses or issues might warrant making copies of the documents and sharing them with key people in advance so that nobody is surprised when the will is executed. Your wishes regarding what should happen if you were to become incapacitated and who is responsible for making decisions on your behalf ought to be shared with all family members and close friends. This way, there can be no question about what you would like done.
>
> **Note: Do not sign copies of a will, or it might qualify as a legal "duplicate original." Write "COPY" in ink on each page just to make sure nobody can claim a copy is the original.
>
> Especially in the case of serious illness and a do-not-resuscitate (DNR) order, a living will, and organ donation, your physicians and other medical providers need to have copies. Your doctors might have their own form for you to fill out related to these matters; be sure to check.

The "who" of a will

Mutual will: This is a plan for your estate that is prepared in conjunction with another person.

For example, sisters Carol and Angie agree to support their disabled brother, Brian, and Grandma Jane. So, they decide that no matter who dies first, 40 percent of either estate goes to Brian, 40 percent goes to Grandma Jane, and the remaining 20 percent goes to other beneficiaries. When the other person dies, 50 percent of her estate goes to Brian, 20 percent goes to Grandma Jane, and the remaining 30 percent goes to other beneficiaries. If Grandma Jane dies before Carol or Angie, her portion goes to Brian.

Joint will: This is one legal document that is for any two people, such as you and your spouse. The problem with this kind of will is that it is irrevocable, which means it cannot be changed after one of the two parties dies. The reason is that all decisions must be made by both people. A lawyer can tell you when this kind of will is a good idea, but most suggest separate wills to avoid complications. Joint wills have been recognized in New York.

Simple will: A single legal document that is written by one person that identifies who you are, your beneficiaries, your executor, the directions you leave for the care of people for whom you are responsible, and the distribution of your assets.

The "what" of a will

Pour over will: This will place some property into a trust that was established while you were still alive.

Testamentary trust will: This will move your assets into one or more trusts after your death. See Chapter 6 for more information on trusts.

The "how" of a will

Holographic will: This is a handwritten document that is signed by you but not witnessed by anyone else. Some states recognize a handwritten will as valid. New York only recognizes holographic wills for people on active military and maritime service. *Chapter 11 provides information on how this works in New York.*

Nuncupative will: Also called an oral will, this is a spoken will. Some states only allow this kind of will if someone is literally on his or her deathbed and it only covers personal property of little or no value. As with holographic wills, New York only recognizes nuncupative wills for active military and maritime service. *This is discussed further in Chapter 11.*

Video will: Only Nevada currently recognizes the option of a video will. Some states will, in extreme circumstances, allow a will to be recorded by a terminally ill person from a deathbed — literally. Recording messages to loved ones might be something you want to do, but they will not be a legal substitute for your last will and testament in New York.

It is important to consider how the will you prepare will complement or conflict with other elements of your estate plan.

• *Did You Know?* •

"Non-traditional" children are becoming as common as the "traditional" kind — the biological offspring of a heterosexual couple. Even though some of those biologics are considered illegitimate when their parents are not legally married, federal and state law typically define children in that traditional sense.

Over time, legally adopted children have become synonymous with biological children in the eyes of the law. But in an era when divorce, infertility, and same-sex couples mean kids become part of a family though in vitro fertilization (IVF), adoptions originating in a foreign country, and stepchildren, inheritance can be a tricky thing.

A child born outside a legally recognized union — in most states, including New York, this is defined as a marriage between a woman and a man — will automatically inherit her/his mother's estate. An inheritance from the biological father is not necessarily automatic. New York does recognize life partners, however.

Many state laws allow a child to inherit from a man who is identified as the father through a paternity test. The father can also marry the mother after the child is born and acknowledge himself as the father of the "out of wedlock" daughter/son. If paternity — the action taken to establish the biological relationship of an adult in a parent-child relationship — is not established, then a child cannot inherit from the estate of the unidentified parent. New York family court has established procedures for paternity actions including do-it-yourself forms.

☑ Watch Out for This

☐ You must legally adopt stepchildren for them to be considered part of your family; if you do not adopt them, and your will directs your estate to fund trust funds for "my children," only those minors who are recognized by the state — not you — as yours will be able to receive a bequest.

☐ A paternity test is the comparison of blood taken from the potential father against a blood sample of the child.

☐ A paternity suit is a legal action that is initiated to establish a man as the biological father of a child.

☐ While the question of paternity is typically associated with the father, a paternity test can be used to establish the biological relationship of a mother as well, in the case of abandonment or other circumstances in which a mother is not clearly identified.

The "Other" Will

Many people prepare a living will at the time they draw up the will for their estate, even though it has nothing to do with your house, car, or checking account. A living will or medical directive is a document in which you spell out the decisions you have made about your medical care while you are still alive. The idea is to decide what kind of measures you want — or do not want — taken on your behalf if you should become incapacitated.

All states — including New York — now recognize living wills, but the documents are not uniform. Some states will only allow living wills to apply to a person who is permanently unconscious or has a terminal illness. Others will allow them for advanced-stage illnesses, such as the final stages of Alzheimer's, when death is not imminent.

To make sure your wishes are followed, you need to understand what is and is not allowed by New York laws. A statutory living will is one that complies with the statutes, or laws, of your state. . The differences between a statutory and nonstatutory living will might seem obvious, but like most legalities, the details can be critical for the will's recognition. A statutory document will likely provide more protection for the physicians and nurses carrying out your wishes. *New York's approach to living wills is covered in Chapter 11.*

Wording is important. A statement such as "I do not want to become a burden to my family," while indicative that you have given the concept some thought, is still vague as to which life-saving measures you do or do not want done for you. Your living will should be specific and address your medical history, so consulting your doctor about what-if scenarios is essential to understanding what kinds of lifesaving measures might be taken to keep you alive. If you have a history of congestive heart failure in your family and have been diagnosed with the same condition, and you do not want extraordinary measures — such as being kept alive by feeding tube or respirator — taken to prolong your life, your wishes must be spelled out.

Another way to make sure your wishes are followed regarding your medical care is to designate a health care power of attorney (HCPA), also known as a medical power of attorney. Your HCPA involves designating a person to make medical decisions for you when you cannot do it for yourself by signing a legal document known as a power of attorney. Many states have laws that allow family members to make some or all of your health care decisions. These family-consent or health-surrogate laws follow a specific order of kinship for who makes a decision; if you are married, your spouse — not your sister — will be your surrogate. Even though the default position of most physicians is to consult the family, having your wishes spelled out in an HCPA relieves your family of having to deal with that issue.

In New York, the concept is enacted through a living will or health care proxy that is used to give someone else the authority to make medical decisions on your behalf. It is similar to a power of attorney.

In general, a durable power of attorney is a document used to give someone else the authority to make medical decisions on your behalf. This kind of power of attorney allows an authorized person to act on behalf of the grantor of that power of attorney.

Making decisions about life-sustaining treatment, artificial nutrition and hydration, and organ donation are the advanced directives most people prepare. A DNR order — do not resuscitate if you appear to have died — is an example of the kind of decision you can make and communicate in your living will. Completing an organ donor card will reinforce your decision to make that gift, if that is important to you.

To avoid confusion or conflict at a later date, make sure your living will is properly executed with witnesses present. Then make sure close family members and friends have copies of the document and understand your wishes. That way, when a medical decision needs to be made, there is not any question about what you would want.

• *Did You Know?* •

The Health Insurance Portability and Accountability Act (HIPAA) is a federal law passed in 1996 that did more than just create more forms for you to sign when you go to the doctor's office. It protects medical insurance coverage for employees when they change or lose their jobs. It also forced the creation and implementation of national standards for conducting electronic medical care transactions for providers, medical insurance companies/plans, and employers. But it also put into place privacy protections that prevent caregivers from sharing your personal information with anyone not explicitly authorized by you.

Questions were raised about the access to private information for someone holding a health care/medical power of attorney: Can that person be given confidential medical information by medical staff in order to make informed decisions, as the incapacitated person expected?

The answer is yes. A form explicitly giving your designated person access to your information is not necessary. The U.S. Department of Health and Human Services confirmed that the power of attorney supersedes the HIPAA privacy requirements.

It is still a good idea to make sure all your medical care providers — primary care physician, eye doctor, dentist, and any specialists — have a copy of your health care/medical power of attorney on file. This can help avoid delays in case of an emergency.

People Speaking for You

After you are no longer able to speak for yourself, others will speak on your behalf. Those individuals you choose to act for you have a host of legal and moral issues to manage, so choosing who will represent you is a serious matter. The lawyer preparing your will and the executor of your will are the two people who will have the most immediate and significant impact on what happens after you are gone. To choose the best people for these tasks, it is important to know what they do.

Wills attorney

The lawyer you work with to draw up your will should be experienced in probate and estate planning. In addition to being well versed in federal law regarding estates, he or she also needs to know what New York requires for a will to be valid/legal. If your estate-planning process includes several planning professionals, such as a CPA or financial planner, then your lawyer also should be someone who works well with others.

The more elusive criteria for choosing your legal representative are those things that give you a sense that you can trust and work with this person. You need to be able to share all the details of your life that go into the composition of your estate. Your wishes for the devise of your property are intensely personal, and you must be able to be complete and candid with your attorney so that he or she will be able to give you the best advice. You also need to be comfortable going back repeatedly to make changes to your will and estate plan, in keeping with changes in your life and sometimes the law.

It is also important that you feel able to communicate comfortably and effectively with the person who will manage your estate.

Executor

After you are gone, you want someone to take care of your estate the way you would. That means finding the right person to follow the necessary steps after you die, such as:

- Guide your will through the probate process to make sure it is accepted as valid. This also means defending the will against any contest challenges.

- Collect, inventory, and safeguard your assets until they are distributed.

- Oversee the transition of bequests to your beneficiaries. This might include a title transfer for a house or making sure a life insurance policy check is made out in the correct name.

- Review, evaluate, and pay any claims against your estate. These include taxes and outstanding bills that are owed.

- Raise the money to pay claims. This can mean selling assets, such as a house or car.

- Prepare and file an accounting of all financial transactions for the court.

- File tax returns and pay taxes.

- Represent the estate in any disputes raised by creditors, heirs, or beneficiaries.

Failure to do any of these things can have serious consequences for the executor, so it is extremely important that the person who agrees to take on this responsibility understands the obligations. You can designate the lawyer this person will use to assist in the probate process.

Although it is impossible to predict how an executor will handle this kind of responsibility, giving careful thought to who will carry out your wishes is important. Because this is such a time-consuming, key responsibility, the law provides for an executor to be paid a fee for services. The executor can agree to waive these fees — as would be the case if he or she is your spouse. The matter of executor fees is something you should discuss with your lawyer as part of your estate-planning process. Similarly, the court approves compensation for lawyers representing estates in the probate process. You should discuss the ramifications of this expense on the estate with your lawyer as well.

Change and Your Will

Simply put, things happen. That is why it is essential to make sure that changes you experience in your life are reflected in your will. Once a will is written, it is not etched in stone — it can be revised or even replaced.

To make a change to a specific portion of your will, you create a codicil. This is a separate legal document that adds to your existing will. It is an easy way to make a few simple changes. When you are older, a codicil is an easy way to protect your will from being challenged due to incompetence. If you only change one part, then the codicil might be successfully challenged, but not the majority of your will.

You might wind up changing your will without even realizing it. If you bequest specific property to someone, such as a boat, but then you sell it, or it sinks during a storm, it will be addressed by the court. No matter what the reason, if property is missing from your estate that is named in your will, then it is considered adeemed. Ademption statutes govern the distribution of your belongings, and the state will take over if items are missing. There are ways to avoid this problem, such as having "back-up" property to serve as a substitute or other provision you may wish to make.

If a beneficiary in your will dies before you do, the gift to that beneficiary is said to have lapsed. If the property exists and no contingent beneficiary is named, then the state steps in if it has an antilapse statute. If your state does not have such a statute, then the property would most likely be covered by the residuary clause, but it is best to check with an attorney to be sure.

Maybe at the time of your death you are carrying a ton of debt that you were going to pay off in the near future. An unexpected departure is something you can plan for in your will, but it takes some planning. The usual method for paying off debt is to sell property in the estate, such as jewelry, antiques, vehicles, or vacation property.

However, if there still is not enough money to take care of those debts, your house might have to be sold, leaving your family homeless. Some states have a homestead exemption statute that protects the family home from being sold. Even this is not a 100 percent guarantee, so work with your estate-planning team to figure out how to address the impact of large debt and other "what if" scenarios.

The following is how the homestead exemption works in New York, under New York Civil Practice Law and Rules section 5206:

1. The value of the home protected is limited to $50,000 "above liens and encumbrances" — meaning equity value of the home not entailed by mortgages and/or liens.

2. The home must be the primary residence and occupied by the debtor.

3. The type of home can be a lot with a house on it; a condominium unit; shares of stock in a cooperative apartment corporation.

4. The exemption does not apply to sale for taxes owed or judgment obtained for the purchase of the home.

5. Exemption continues after the death of the person "in whose favor the property was exempted" for the benefit of the deceased's surviving spouse and children, and lasts until the youngest child reaches age of majority and until the surviving spouse dies.

6. A home with equity worth more than $50,000 does not lose the exemption but it can be sold and the amount over $50,000 collected against debt.

7. Dedicated burial grounds are also exempt from judgment creditors.

CHAPTER 6
Trusts

The image many people have of a child with a trust fund is someone with access to all the money necessary to pay for a college education, an extended tour of Europe, or a carefree future without money problems. The truth of the matter is that you do not have to be independently wealthy to set up a trust, and their uses are significantly more diverse than the aforementioned stereotype.

The basic idea behind a trust is to set aside specific property for specific people or institutions so that you, not the courts, decide what will happen to your estate. Knowing what you want to put into the trust, who benefits from the trust, and the price to be paid — set-up fees, taxes, time — is essential to making sure you choose the right trust.

There are at least a dozen different kinds of trusts with various combinations of legal and tax implications, so there is no such thing as a "standard" trust. A book like this one can help you learn what a trust is, but any "one-size-fits-all" trust template is a disaster waiting to happen.

Each trust is customized to meet the needs of the individual — that is what makes a trust so attractive and difficult. Laws and tax requirements at the federal and state level are constantly changing, and so are your needs. With the extremely real possibility that your trust could end up in probate or in the hands of the government, it is essential to work with an estate planner and lawyer to make sure you have the proper documents in place so that your trust is legal and enforceable.

To make sure the outcome you want is the one you get, learn what a trust is, its benefits, and its drawbacks. The steps to set up a trust and the elements of a trust can be easy enough to understand: Identify what property will be included, who benefits, who manages the trust, tax implications for all the people involved, and how the law governs all that activity. The tricky part is learning about the different kinds of trusts and matching them up with your wishes.

What is a Trust?

A trust is a legal arrangement that involves the transfer of property from the original owner to a person or a company for the purpose of holding and maintaining the property until it is handed over to the beneficiary — the individual or institution designated to receive the property.

It seems straightforward enough — until you get into the many legal terms, people, laws, and taxes that go into the creation of a trust. With many interchangeable terms, some of which are as confusing as the Greek or Roman terms from which they originated, a list of who is who and what is what is helpful. The following situation will assist you with recognizing the roles each person plays in a trust.

People: Aunt Tara wants to set up a trust for her house so that her niece Betsy will have a place to set up her veterinary clinic after she finishes her education. However, she does not know when Betsy will graduate, so she wants her grandson Charles to take care of the place if she — Aunt Tara — dies. In case something happens to Charles, his wife, Kim, will take on that responsibility.

- **Trustor** (Aunt Tara): The person who sets up the trust. Other names commonly used are creator, donor, settlor, or grantor.

- **Beneficiary** (Betsy): The individual(s) or group(s) that will receive the property in the trust. This can be a single person, a group of people, one group, several groups, or a combination of any of these.

- **Trustee** (Charles): The person or company that will oversee or manage the trust once it is established. This person (or group) will make sure the property in the trust is safe and in good order until it is turned over to the beneficiary. This includes paying any taxes, performing repairs, or doing anything else an owner would do. The trustee is obligated to carry out the terms of the trust and can be paid for this effort, if terms for this are included in the trust language.

- **Successor trustee** (Kim): Someone who will step in if the primary trustee is unable to serve or cannot continue to manage your trust. This person will have the same legal obligations for managing the trust as the original trustee, should the successor assume the management responsibilities.

The individual or company designated to serve as trustee carries a significant amount of responsibility and needs to be someone you trust implicitly. The potential for a conflict of interest or being swayed by the temptation to do something inappropriate — such as stealing from the trust or neglecting the work — needs to be considered. Putting language in the trust documents that spells out the responsibilities of the trustees is essential, and creating a mechanism of oversight and removal will also prevent your heirs from losing what is supposed to be theirs.

Things and strings: Aunt Tara's housesits on 4 acres of land with an out-building to store the lawn tractor and other equipment. Over the years, she sold the other 12 acres, so she invested the money into a mutual fund. Aunt Tara had her lawyer set up a trust fund that gives Betsy the interest from the mutual fund to pay tuition when it is due in the fall, but Aunt Tara's mutual fund will not go to Betsy until she graduates from college. The house in the care of Charles will also go to Betsy after she graduates.

- **Property**: Anything you want to give to other people, also referred to as principal. There are all kinds of legal terms for the "stuff" you own, and you have to make sure you use the right words to identify everything from money in a safe or checking account to a rocking chair or commemorative baseball. This can be real property or real estate (10-acre farm), tangible personal property (the things you can touch, such as a lawn tractor and other equipment), or intangible personal property (financial assets, such as certificates of deposit).

- **Trust agreement**: The legal document that spells out the terms of a trust, including the people and conditions and the rules that must be followed. Some are state or federal laws, and others are specific conditions (trust fund).

- **Funding a trust**: The placement of property in a trust; that same property will be called trust principal once it is under the auspices of the trust agreement.

- **Provisions**: The clauses that spell out how you want your wishes carried out. Distribution provisions will identify to whom the income will be given and the frequency of those distributions (pay tuition when it is due in the fall). Special provisions encompass all requirements that are unique to the beneficiary or the assets (graduates from college).

- **Legal title**: This gives the trustee ownership of the property in the trust for the duration of the trustee's responsibility (house in Charles's care).

- **Beneficial title**: Also known as equitable title, this is the right of the person or institution to take possession of or benefit from the property in the trust (goes to Betsy).

The plan can be incredibly clear, but whether the end result matches that plan depends on the kind of trust you choose, the way the documents are worded, and the way the people involved carry out their tasks. It is easier to make mistakes than it is to get it right, and those mistakes can be costly for loved ones. If you are not careful, they can inherit a big mess instead of the things you want them to have.

One way to avoid such a mess is to carefully choose a trustee who will carry out your wishes and do so legally. Being a trustee is more than just whipping out a checkbook and signing a few papers now and then.

Talking to Your Estate Planner about Trusts

Before you sit down with your estate planner, take some time to think about the questions you have regarding your life circumstances. Here are a few questions to keep in mind:

- What are the tax consequences for this trust? What about capital gains?
- What happens to the "leftovers" in a trust — cash, property, and everything else?
- Will there be a problem if the trust beneficiary dies before you do?
- What are the tax consequences for this trust? What about capital gains?
- What happens to the "leftovers" in a trust — cash, property, and everything else?

- Will there be a problem if the trust beneficiary dies before you do?
- What happens if the terms of a trust are not met — e.g., Bobby quits school before his educational trust is spent?
- When does a specific use trust terminate — for example, if Aunt Mimi's disability trust is still in place after she dies?
- What happens to an irrevocable trust if the situation changes?
- What are the advantages and disadvantages for a single person in setting up a trust?
- What happens if some of the property in your trust is community property and you divorce?
- If you end up divorced, what happens to the education trust fund that Mom and Dad are funding for little Suzy?

Things to consider...

An estate planner can also help you address some of the unexpected or unusual life circumstances that might not be on your mind. There are also legal ramifications for your death that might not come up during your life. For example, unmarried partners do not get the same automatic consideration that a legally married couple has. A qualified terminable interest property trust (QTIP) is not an option for a couple who does not have a legally documented marriage.

Some other things that affect the legality and terms of a trust include:

- Foreign-born spouse
- Non-biological "family" members
- Same-sex couples
- Living together — as opposed to a formal or common-law marriage
- Adoption
- Pets
- Divorce
- Multiple marriages — offspring and spouses
- Incapacitation
- Medical condition / serious illness
- Permanent disability
- Natural disaster affecting property
- Stock / real estate market crash

Types of Trusts

A trust can be set up to take effect while you are alive (inter vivos), or it can take effect after you die (testamentary). Some can be changed (revocable), and some cannot be changed no matter what (irrevocable). Some trusts can be terminated or ended, while others cannot. The purpose of a trust can result in a tax exemption or a higher tax rate, depending on what the current tax law allows.

There are trusts for yourself and trusts for other people, and many of the reasons for setting up either kind are the same — getting tax benefits, staying out of probate court, protecting assets from creditors, or making sure money is available "just in case" for matters like education, severe illness, or a disability. Considering all life's possibilities to decide which trust(s) would be helpful is a daunting task. Another way to look at the situation is to consider the kinds of trusts that already exist and have defined legal and tax consequences.

Trusts fall into a number of categories that can be described by different criteria. One criterion is the beneficiary. A marital-dedicational trust is specific to the surviving, legal spouse of the deceased. A bypass trust will transfer property to someone other than your spouse, such as a child or grandchild, but allow him to still benefit from the property in the trust. Some states, including New York, even allow you to create a trust for your pets.

Another criterion is the reason for the trust. If you want to protect the beneficiary's property so that it is available for a specific reason when it is needed, you would use a protective trust. A discretionary trust gives the trustee the ability to distribute income and property to a variety of beneficiaries; he or she also has the option to control the distributions to a single beneficiary as he or she decides is appropriate. That offers some flexibility, as does a dynasty trust; also known as a wealth trust, it can last for several generations, or be set up to never end. This kind of trust helps people with a vast amount of wealth control the distribution of that money and property over a long period of time. However, many states limit non-charitable trusts to 90 years.

The overarching requirements of a trust create yet another group. A split-interest means more than one individual benefits from the trust: One person or charity would have an interest in the trust for a specific period of time, and then another person or charity receives the property that remains. A support trust requires a trustee to pay only the income and property necessary to cover the cost of education or assistance, such as health care or nursing home fees, of the beneficiaries.

Some trusts are automatically irrevocable, so you have to make sure you know what you are signing before you pick up the pen. However, many trusts can be set up as revocable or irrevocable, with a variety of conditions that put the trust into one of the categories already defined by tax law. These laws continue changing to keep up with the creative efforts to avoid taxes.

These conditions and restrictions make it important to consult an estate-planning specialist to discuss the trust options that will help you achieve your goals and understand the tax implications of your choices.

The following is a list of the different types of trusts:

- **Burial trust**: Provides the funds necessary to cover the cost of your burial or cremation arrangements. This can be a revocable trust, but after your death, it becomes irrevocable, and the trust cannot be used for anything else.

- **Charitable trust**: Offers the benefits of tax-free gifts for the donor. A charitable remainder trust gives gifts of interest income that are paid to specific beneficiaries such as your spouse for a specific period of time; at the end of that time period, a charity receives whatever is left in the trust. A charitable lead trust, or a front trust, gives the charity a specific gift before all other beneficiaries receive anything. These are both split-interest trusts. Split-interest trusts make distributions to both charitable and noncharitable beneficiaries, while providing tax benefits to their donor.

- **Crummey trust**: An exceedingly complicated trust normally set up in conjunction with an irrevocable life insurance trust to make the payments for a life insurance policy. This is the kind of trust that requires an estate-planning attorney.

- **Educational trust**: This is a kind of protective trust that sets aside money specifically for education-related expenses, such as tuition or training fees, books, or supplies. These trusts regularly include provisions to stop payments if the student drops out of school or flunks many classes.

- **Generation-skipping transfer trust (GSTT)**: A tax-saving trust designed to benefit multiple generations after you are gone.

- **Grantor-retained trusts**: These are irrevocable and non-charitable, which means they cannot be changed and the beneficiary is not a charity. There are three common types: A grantor-retained annuity trust (GRAT) gives a fixed amount of money at predetermined times, often at regularly scheduled intervals; a grantor-retained unit trust (GRUT) pays a specific percentage to the beneficiary; and a grantor-retained incomes trust (GRIT) designates specific people to receive certain property, such as stocks or a house, but the income or use of the property stays with you until your death.

- **Living trust**: Created while you are still alive, this trust allows you to be the grantor, trustee, and beneficiary, if you choose.

- **Marital dedication trust**: Puts property into a trust that is exclusively for your spouse, who decides what happens to the property after your death.

- **Minor trust**: A way to give gifts to minors that avoids the gift tax and keeps the property safe until the minor becomes an adult and can take ownership of the trust.

- **QTIP**: A qualified terminable interest property trust is a marital deduction trust. However, instead of your spouse's deciding who gets the property after your death, the grantor makes that decision.

- **Spendthrift trust**: A trust that is set up for someone who will not be able to handle their own affairs, e.g., someone who is mentally incompetent or might have financial problems and needs protection from creditors. The beneficiary does not own the property in the trust, just the payments that are made from the trust.

- **Special needs trust**: A support trust for a disabled person under the age of 65 (you or anyone else), this trust makes payments on the beneficiary's behalf, as required by the state as reimbursement. After the beneficiary dies, the property in the trust is paid to other beneficiaries. This trust is designed to protect your property from seizure by the government or a creditor seeking reimbursement.

- **Supplemental needs trust**: A support trust designed to provide income to a handicapped, elderly, or disabled person to supplement their income, but is structured in a way that does not reduce or jeopardize the eligibility of that person to receive public or private benefits. This trust is designed to protect your property from seizure by the government or a creditor seeking reimbursement.

- **Testamentary trust**: Created by the terms of your will after your death.

- **Totten trust**: This is a bank account that, upon your death, immediately passes to the named beneficiary.

There are also special trusts for specific things such as real estate, life insurance, or pension benefits. Choosing which trust will meet your needs and those of your estate is a difficult process. This information is a way for you to familiarize yourself with the choices that are out there, but an estate-planning specialist is the best person to help you decide whether you need a trust and which one will be the best choice.

• *Did You Know?* •

If you have a modest estate, but you still want your minor children to inherit your property, you can use the Uniform Transfer for Minors Act (UTMA) or the Uniform Gift to Minors Act (UGMA). Most states, including New York, have adopted this legislation, which allows you to create a custodian account for a minor.

A custodian account, which can be in the form of a trust, allows you to deposit money or property in an account set up by a bank or a brokerage firm. You name yourself as the custodian — trustee — of the account while you are alive and name a successor to take over those responsibilities after you die. This new custodian will serve in that capacity until the child reaches 18, 21, or 25, depending on the state law.

☑ Watch Out for This

☐ Some states hand over the ownership of the account to the child when he or she turns 18, and you have no say after that.

☐ Accounts for children over the age of 13 are subject to federal income tax at the children's rate. This will most certainly be lower than your tax rate, but the implications of this need to be considered.

☐ If you create an UGMA or UTMA account, this can reduce the amount of court paperwork and supervision, thereby lowering estate costs.

☐ Even if you create this kind of account, you must still name a legal guardian for your children in your will. The legal guardian can also be custodian of this kind of account, but naming a custodian of an account is not the same as naming a legal guardian.

Pros and Cons of Forming a Trust

Trusts provide some excellent benefits, but they are not the perfect solution for everything. One benefit is that some trusts can reduce the amount of taxes that have to be paid before and after you die. However, if your trust is not set up properly, it might have to pay income tax. A trust can protect your assets from your creditors or those of your beneficiaries, but only if it is set up properly.

More private than a will, which becomes public record upon your death and makes the details of your estate available to anyone who wants access, a trust can keep others out of your personal business. In many cases, a trust can help keep your estate out of probate court, and it is more difficult to contest a trust than a will. The flexibility of a trust allows you to make changes and can even help with financial issues if you become disabled during your life.

The downside is that it costs money to set up a trust, and there are numerous scams out there, both foreign and domestic. So, if you are not careful, you could wind up losing the property you want to go to your loved ones and charity. There also is the possibility that your trustee will abscond with the contents of the trusts and head for a non-extradition country.

Whether trusts are worth all the hassle and potential risk is up to you — and that is why is it essential to work with estate-planning specialists when setting up any trust(s).

The Dos and Don'ts for Trusts

The following tips are things to consider when you are preparing your trust:

- Think of choosing a trust as a dry run for your estate planning. Consider all possible life scenarios and how a trust will or will not help those situations.

- When setting up a trust or trusts, do them all at once so that you can save a few dollars — with any luck — and make sure none of them conflict with the others.

- Put all trust agreements in writing.

- Make sure the proper legal language is used in every agreement.

- Clearly define the trustee responsibilities and obligations. A "passive" trust, which does not define these things, might not be recognized by a court as a trust.

- Clearly identify beneficiaries.

- Clearly define the property in the trust. "Everything in the dining room" is an example of what not to do.

- Make sure the property you put into a trust will meet the needs you identify. $100,000 to pay for a college education in the year 2100 might not be enough.

- Carefully choose a trustee who will execute your wishes, take care of all legal obligations, and is willing to take on all those duties.

- Keep an eye on the content and value of each trust over time — fluctuating market conditions and changes in your life might leave a trust underfunded, or may be obsolete.

Notes about other information you want to learn: _____
_____
_____
_____
_____

Obligations of the Trustee — New York

A trustee of a trust holds what is called a fiduciary duty to manage the trust assets and distributions with due care, according to the intent of the trust's creator as detailed in the trust's governing documents and in the best interests of the trust according to that intent and good judgment. The trustee cannot lawfully use the trust for his or her own personal gain or interest or that of someone who is not a legitimate beneficiary of the trust.

New York Code EPT section 11-2.3 is the Prudent Investor Act, which governs the role of the trustee. The statute requires a trustee to execute his or her duties according to the "prudent investor standard" unless the trust instrument expressly provides otherwise. In simple terms, the prudent investor standard does not hold a trustee accountable for outcome or performance of investments made on behalf of the trust so long as the trustee pursues an "overall investment strategy to enable the trustee to make appropriate present and future distributions to or for the benefit of the beneficiaries under the governing instrument, in accordance with risk and return objectives reasonably suited to the entire portfolio." *The complete text of New York's Prudent Investor Act is included in Appendix C of this book.*

Note that the guidelines provided by this statute are subordinate to guidelines and covenants contained in the trust instrument itself. This means that when you set up a trust you have the ability to determine how you want the trustee to act on behalf of the trust. This is not something to undertake casually or uninformed. Whether you are comfortable with the Prudent Investor Act standard or want to be more specific in your direction when creating the trust is a conclusion you should reach with advice of experienced New York legal counsel.

CHAPTER 7

Insurance

Insurance is one part of your estate plan, and it can be an especially effective part if you have good information and advice tailored to your needs, not those of the person pushing papers across the desk for you to sign. How you want to make that money work for you should guide your shopping and decision-making. Consider:

- **Funeral expenses**: On average, these range from $5,000 - $8,000 but can go much higher.

- **Grief money**: Supports your family during their grieving period so they do not have to rush back to work to cover the bills.

- **Debts**: Cover the cost of money you owe to others so that it does not reduce the size of your estate.

- **Estate costs**: Ready cash to cover estate taxes and costs for distributing your estate and provide a stipend for your executor.

- **Lost income**: Gives your family access to some of the income you would have earned.

- **Education funds**: Money for school, now or in the future.

- **Funding a trust**: This will add to the property in the trust and be distributed like all the other assets in that trust.

- **Taxes**: Giving money to your "probate estate" is a way to make sure your estate has enough money to cover tax payment to state and federal tax collectors.

For a rather small investment, you can provide your beneficiaries with a substantial amount of money, if you choose carefully.

When you die, the insurance company that holds your life insurance policy cuts a check to your spouse, children, or parents, but there is much more to know, including the following:

- If the beneficiary of your policy dies before you do, the money goes into probate.

- An insurance policy that invests in the stock market might actually lose value, leaving your beneficiaries with less money.

- A serious illness can devastate the assets of your estate, which means the life insurance you wanted to support your family could end up in the hands of creditors instead.

Insurance, like most things in life, is not quite as simple as it once was — or as sales reps like to make it appear. The kind of insurance you have when you are alive can affect your estate as much as the insurance you have for after your death, so this is where the here-and-now affects the future.

Insurance, simply defined, is a method to protect the things we value most. Some insurance is mandated by law (automobile insurance), while some is considered essential (health insurance, although this is also becoming mandated by law), and other kinds are considered a luxury (disability and long-term care). What kind and how much insurance any individual needs is based upon individual circumstances. If you do not have a $20 million country estate, it is not likely that you are going to need the kind of liability insurance that would protect you against a lawsuit brought by someone who stayed for the weekend and was hurt while riding a horse from your stable.

As part of your overall estate plan, insurance can accomplish some of the more conventional goals people have, such as providing cash to pay taxes so that your family does not have to sell property to settle with Uncle Sam. What is slightly more uncommon is considering the impact a permanent disability can have on the assets of your estate and how you will maintain that estate until it is passed on to someone else.

Thinking about insurance before you need it is the best way to consider the host of options and tangle of details and conditions related to each. This requires much "what if" speculation on your part, but educated guesses are possible when you make time to let your imagination run free.

Insurance for Here and Now

Most insurance commercials focus on the worst-case scenario to scare you into buying peace of mind. Though horrible, these situations are exactly what you need to consider. While not fun, considering the effects of a serious illness, debilitating accident, or natural disaster can point you in the right directions for figuring out your insurance needs.

Medical insurance

Frequently referred to as health insurance by those who sell it, the insurance that covers medical costs is almost never used when you are healthy — but you always have to whip out that benefits card when you fill a prescription for strep throat, have a heart attack, or break a bone.

The first question you need to consider is whether your insurance policy will cover your bills when you truly need it to, because if your insurance does not pay, you will have to. That payment can be high enough to wipe out your savings, not to mention any other assets you have built up over time. What most people consider is the amount that is deducted from every paycheck week after week, not the tens of thousands of dollars a hospital will try to collect from you after you have hit your "maximum lifetime benefit."

Even if your family has no history of colon cancer, breast cancer, heart attack, or even high cholesterol, you can still be involved in a workplace accident or a horrible car crash that is not your fault, or contract a rare virus on the only trip you ever take out of the country. Anyone who has children or knows someone who has children knows that trips to the emergency room and doctor's office are the rule, not the exception.

A simple cold going around school can land your child in an intensive care unit (ICU) with walking pneumonia — will your insurance cover a stay in a pediatric ICU? What if your child requires hospitalization while out of state visiting relatives? Knowing the terms of your medical insurance coverage, beyond the monthly premium, is an essential part of your estate planning. A few simple things to check are:

- What is the maximum lifetime benefit per person? Per policy?

- What serious illnesses are not covered?

- How is a "pre-existing condition" defined, and can that be excluded from your coverage?

- Do you have "out-of-network" coverage? Can you purchase additional coverage if you are going to travel out of your network area? Out of the country?

- What about medical care provided outside the United States — can you get reimbursed for those costs?

- When can you make changes to your coverage?

After you find the answers to these questions, compare the information against your family medical history — do any of the "not covered" illnesses run in your family? Also, consider what is on the horizon for your family, such as a child going to study abroad for a year or an overweight spouse starting a new exercise program without consulting a doctor. Paying a slightly higher premium now for better coverage can prevent some devastating bills later.

A person who receives a diagnosis of cancer typically does not begin thinking about funding a family trip to Bermuda; he is thinking about extensive treatments, not being able to coach Little League, and maybe being unable to work for an extended period of time. Do not leave everything in the hands of your insurance agent. Preparing for these "what-if" situations is your job.

Disability insurance

A disability insurance policy will make payments to you to cover living expenses and replace your lost income as a result of your inability to hold a job. So, if you cannot work because you are sick, get hurt, or for some other reason, this insurance will replace some of your lost income. Imagine what could happen to your savings if you are stuck at home in bed, but the mortgage payment, utilities bills, and furnace repair invoices keep coming.

Your ability to leave anything for your loved ones after you are gone is largely dependent upon the work you do while you are alive. Though disability insurance will not replace 100 percent of your income, it would certainly be better than nothing. The question is whether the conditions and restrictions make it a worthwhile investment for you. If you feel it is a good idea, determine what kind of disability insurance will meet your needs.

There are many different disability plans out there, but they fall into two types: short- or long-term. Short-term disability provides benefits for about three months; some plans go a little longer, but they are a temporary fix. Long-term disability can provide benefits for years but does eventually end — frequently at 65, when you become eligible for social security. The benefits are as varied as the plans available. Some details to look for include:

- **When the policy goes into effect**: Some policies do not begin to make payments until you have been out of work for a specific period of time; they do not make payments the moment you are disabled.

- **How payments are calculated**: Some policies replace a percentage of your income, on average ranging from 50-75 percent.

- **Definition of disability**: You might have to be unable to work at any job, or payments might be made if you are not able to work in your chosen profession.

- **Premium payments**: How they are calculated can depend on the percentage of income replaced — more money means a higher premium — or some other criterion.

The federal government also provides a social security disability benefit for which you might be eligible. But if you think getting only 50 percent of your income reimbursed is not enough, do not count on the government to offer a 100 percent replacement.

While short-term disability can help you through a rough time, long-term disability is going to have a direct impact on your estate plan. A serious injury not only has the potential to rack up major medical bills not covered by health insurance, but it can also eliminate the possibility of future investments and jeopardize your ability to pay life insurance and other premiums.

Long-term care insurance

The difference between long-term disability and long-term care insurance is that the latter provides payments to cover the cost of medical care. In-home nursing or nursing home fees are examples of what might be covered. While this might bring to mind 89-year-old Aunt Mary who could fall and break her hip, this coverage is for any debilitating injury suffered by anyone at any age.

If you fall at work and injure your back so badly that you require surgery and months of physical therapy so you can walk again, your medical insurance might not be enough to cover the entire cost. Again, it is important to understand what the policy will and will not cover and when the payments will begin. If you max out your medical insurance, but your long-term care insurance does not kick in for a year, if ever, the assets in your estate could be in jeopardy.

Looking into all these details before you need to use your insurance is the best way to learn what you need to know. Do not leave it to your family to sort out.

Homeowner's/renter's insurance

If your house is your biggest asset, then protecting it is a no-brainer. The list of possible disasters can keep homeowners up all night immediately before and after buying a house. There is nothing like a down payment and an hour's worth of signing papers to make you realize what is on the line if something goes wrong. Banks are not in the habit of saying, "Your house burned down? Well, then, let's just tear up those loan papers."

Even if you do not own a home, that lease you signed is a legally binding agreement. If you are robbed or the pipes in the apartment above add a waterfall feature to your living room, you are still going to have to pay your rent, and the antique books you wanted to give to niece Amy will not be worth the paper composing the pulp they will resemble.

Making sure you can recoup the loss of your property — both real estate and the things you have to move in boxes — is essential if your estate is to have any value after a disaster, natural or otherwise. Fire, flood, earthquake, tornadoes, snow caving in a roof, wind damage, or anything else you can think of that might possibly damage your home and its contents are the factors to consider when purchasing insurance.

There are some homeowners' policies that will pay off the balance of a home mortgage, leaving the bulk of your estate to replace your income if you do not want your family to worry about money after you are gone. Before signing on that dotted line, find out the circumstances under which the policy might not pay off the mortgage. Just because you die does not mean they will pay up.

Automobile insurance

An antique or exotic car collection would warrant an automobile insurance policy with special coverage for the replacement of such a rare vehicle, as opposed to what the average driver needs. That kind of insurance is important to have if your car collection does not fit on a shelf in the family room, but for everyday driving, there are some basic minimums that everyone needs.

If you lease a car, then you know that the leasing agency requires specific limits for personal injury and liability. New York also requires a minimum amount of insurance coverage to legally drive your car — if you have no insurance, you can have your driver's license suspended or revoked. None of this is likely to be a surprise; what might become a surprise is what happens if you get sued or agree to a settlement that results from an automobile accident and you do not have insurance.

If you have teenagers starting to drive, you know your premiums are going to go up. Car rental agencies figured out the risk of young drivers a long time ago; you have to be 25 to sign a car rental agreement, which is a point not to forget when you have to add another driver to your policy. Remember to check into the per-accident and per-person payout amounts as well — they make a difference.

Car insurance only pays out as much as the limits in your policy. If you want a cheap premium and do not bother to look at what those payouts are, you could end up having to pay a considerable sum. Getting your hands on hundreds of thousands of dollars is not easy for most people, so part of your estate planning is checking into your automobile coverage and deciding whether it is adequate.

Umbrella liability insurance

This kind of policy provides added protection for your property that goes beyond homeowner's, renter's, automobile, or any other kind of insurance. If the person you rear-end at a red light thinks you have a good amount of money, he might stop by the We-Will-Sue-For-You law firm with dollar signs in his eyes. It is not fair that you should have to defend yourself against a frivolous lawsuit, but better that than losing your house or other property because you did not have adequate protection.

When looking into this kind of insurance, it is important to know what is and is not covered. Look for loopholes that will allow the insurance company to wiggle out of paying a claim.

An umbrella policy is not going to be necessary for everyone, but it is often essential to estate planning for people with a high-value estate because they have plenty to lose before they have a chance to pass it on. An insurance agent who tells you anything to the contrary needs to be crossed off your list.

Shopping around for an insurance agent you can trust is going to take some time, but the benefits are valuable. Making sense of all the possible options and understanding the fine print of all those options — not to mention the legalities of making changes and still having your beneficiaries receive what you expect them to — is only going to happen if you do your homework.

Details, Details

It is all about the details when it comes to any kind of insurance, so be sure to ask plenty of questions — and be extremely clear about what can, might, should, and will not happen related to your policies. Ask the hard questions, and do not accept anything less than a full response:

- Under what circumstances will the benefit not be paid? Find out all degrees of risk, including the worst-case scenario.

- Which of my assets are at risk, and from what?

- What kinds of safety nets can insurance provide?

- What kind of insurance does not have a good cost/benefit balance, considering the details of my estate?

- What amount of coverage is excessive for my situation?

- Are there varying degrees of risk among my possible choices? If so, what are they?

- Why would my estate-planning team reject your recommendation?

Policies

With so many options, selecting what you need can be difficult. Check off those you think you might like to include in your estate plan, and then work with an agent to determine whether you need this kind of coverage.

While you are alive:

_____ Medical

_____ Dental

_____ Vision

_____ Disability — long-term

_____ Disability — short-term

_____ Long-term care

_____ Homeowner's/Renter's

_____ Car

_____ Umbrella liability

After death:

_____ Life

_____ Whole life

_____ Universal life

_____ Joint first-to-die or second-to-die

_____ Term life insurance

_____ Annual renewable

_____ Decreasing

_____ Level

_____ Group

_____ Funeral/burial

Insurance for After You Are Gone

Some insurance agents will tell you that all you need is plenty of life insurance to make sure your loved ones are taken care of. However, insurance is not that simple. As with wills and trusts, there are many variations on this protection theme. The following are different types of life insurance:

- **Whole life**: Sometimes called cash-value life insurance, this is the kind of policy most people know: After being qualified — smoker/non-smoker, desk jockey/bungee jumper, age 25/age 75 — the insured person pays a monthly premium on a policy that will, upon his or her death, pay a predetermined, fixed amount of money to his or her beneficiaries. A portion of the fixed (it will never go up or down) premium is invested, another portion is placed into an account — like a savings account — and that cash value is accessible to the policy owner. It can be borrowed against as a loan, or the cash can be taken as the proceeds of the policy instead of the death benefit payout.

  ▶ *Universal life*: A kind of whole life policy that guarantees a minimum return, but the value of the policy can go up or down. If the policy makes more money, the return might be high enough to cover your premium payments.

  ▶ *Joint first-to-die or second-to-die*: Just like it sounds, this is a policy held by two people, and the beneficiary is paid after the first person or second person dies. You decide the payout when you set the terms of the policy.

- **Term life insurance**: Carries an annual premium and pays a specified death benefit to the beneficiary, but it does not have a cash value, so you cannot borrow money from it. The only payment made is to the beneficiary. The premium is based on the amount of insurance you purchase — what will be paid out after your death — and how old you are: Younger people pay less and, as they get older, their premiums rise accordingly. If you stop paying premiums, the death benefit is not paid. There are a number of different kinds of term policies available:

▶ ***Annual renewable***: A policy that has an annual premium and can be renewed from year to year. Be sure you understand the renewal rights before signing.

▶ ***Decreasing***: Premiums remain the same, but the benefit decreases over time. For example, if you purchase this kind of insurance to pay off your debts after you die — also known as mortgage or credit term insurance — the mortgage you want to insure is $250,000 at the time you purchase the insurance, but the mortgage value when you die is $150,000; the policy pays $150,000. This kind of insurance is recommended only for those who cannot get any other kind of insurance.

▶ ***Level***: Coverage is guaranteed for a specific period of time, or term, such as five, ten, or 20 years at a specific premium. The premium will remain for the five-year period, but at year six, it will go up and remain at that rate through the tenth year, continuing in that direction.

▶ ***Group***: Employers frequently purchase a term life policy for each employee as an added benefit. Employees get an exceptionally low rate, and there is no income tax on the premiums for the first $50,000 of coverage.

• *Did You Know?* •

In order to receive the death benefit from a life insurance policy, a death certificate for the policy holder is required as proof of death.

The most expedient way for your executor to obtain a copy is through the mortuary or other institution that is responsible for handling the body of the deceased. Copies can also be obtained from the county health department.

☑ Watch Out for This!

☐ Authorized copies of a death certificate are needed to provide proof of death. As with a birth certificate, you cannot just reproduce a few dozen at your local copy center.

☐ Obtain several copies of the death certificate. Most institutions that require a certificate for proof will retain it for their files.

☐ Money will change hands, so call the county health department to find out the current fee.

Beneficiaries

No matter what type of insurance you decide to purchase, you can choose different beneficiaries depending on what the policy is going to do. To start, consider the goal of the policy, per the opening section of this chapter, and who will need or use that money for that purpose. A life insurance policy that is specifically set up to give your family time to grieve might name your spouse as the beneficiary because he or she, not your estate, will pay the utility bills and buy the groceries.

Regardless of whom you name as the beneficiary, it is important to name an alternative beneficiary. If the first beneficiary dies before you or declines the gift, the second person or institution named will receive the benefit. If the death benefit goes unclaimed, then it is added to your estate and heads to probate for distribution by the court. Creditors and others may get more of the money than family, friends, or a charity you wish to support depending on what is owed at the time of your death.

While there might be tax implications for insurance beneficiaries in certain circumstances, in general, a lump sum life insurance policy payout is not taxable income. There can be exceptions. For example, interest accrued above the death benefit value that is included in the lump sum payout will be taxable. If the beneficiary is your estate (whether by intention or default for lack of viable beneficiary at the time of your death), meaning that the proceeds are paid into your probate estate, then the proceeds become subject to estate tax and/or inheritance tax rules. When it comes to taxes on benefits, whether insurance or another form of gift, make no assumptions. Get up-to-the minute tax advice.

CASE STUDY: INSURANCE: MORE THAN LIFE COVERAGE

Linda Horn
Chief Executive Officer
Capital Concepts
linda@capitalconcepts.net
www.capitalconcepts.net

Some people only buy insurance, and others diversify their investments. What is the benefit of having a large amount of insurance?

Tax-free income to your family or a charity is a benefit. Proceeds from a policy are often used to provide additional funds to pay the estate taxes. Should you own a business or farm, insurance becomes critical to paying federal and state estate tax, due within nine months of your death. Or perhaps you wish to leave a legacy for future generations or name a charity to continue your legacy.

What are the drawbacks of a large amount of insurance?

The premium payment should never create a financial hardship. After all, life is about living.

Under what circumstance might an insurance company not pay out a death benefit on various types of insurance? (e.g., whole life, term life, accidental death)

During the first two years from the issue date, the policy can be contested for suicides or false statements on the application about known medical history that can be attributed to your death. After two years, or if the above does not apply, all claims are paid.

How is disability insurance a valuable part of estate planning?

Disability is often overlooked, when in fact you have six times the probability of becoming disabled while on the job than of dying on the job. Your largest asset is your income. Protecting your income far exceeds your home, yet we would never consider having no homeowner's coverage.

What other types of insurance, beyond life, are important to an estate plan?

Long-term care insurance is an essential part of your plan. Should you need long-term care, such as in a nursing home or assisted-living facility, your assets will quickly be diminished, and little will be left for your spouse or children. Waiting until you know you need it is like insuring your home when it is on fire; you cannot get it, and if you could, it would be very expensive.

What are the benefits of working with an insurance professional?

If you are doing or have done your job of saving properly, a full-time professional is as necessary as the family doctor. A financial advisor works full-time for many years to gain the expertise to get you to your final destination with as few bumps in the road as possible. Approximately 95 percent of do-it-your-selfers lose money, while the use of a professional is just the reverse. The discipline of a balanced approach to risk management and investment will pay off. A good advisor will make you far more money than you ever pay them. Their access to information alone is worth the investment. You do not drill your own teeth or cut your own hair, so why on earth would you invest your life savings with an amateur?

How does a person go about choosing an insurance professional? What characteristics or experience should a potential client look for?

First, ask trusted friends for their recommendations. Second, ask the advisor about their training, years of experience, education, and designations. What is their investment track record and philosophy? Do they share your values and understand you and your goals? Ask for a list of clients you can speak with. And, last, go with your gut.

CHAPTER 8
Retirement Accounts

The "golden years" is public relations speak for that time in your life when your hair might be white or gray, you do not have to set your alarm clock to get up in the morning, and you get to reinvent yourself and have some fun.

People who have access to some kind of pension plan or retirement fund can enjoy traveling, recreation, spoiling family, or even taking on a new enterprise. Some who might have done a little saving for retirement and reach the age of 65 — or 67, if you were born after 1960 — can consider their social security income as extra money, not essential for day-to-day living expenses. The group nobody wants to be in is the one that has little or nothing set aside for retirement, because the monthly payment from social security — $1,000 - $2,500 — almost certainly is not going to be enough to live on.

Such scenarios have implications for your estate planning. Most retirement planning sets a target for how much money you think you will need when you retire so that you can finally stop working. However, that plan is an estimate, and things can happen that mean you have more or less money than is needed.

As the current economy is teaching us, income does not necessarily commensurate with the cost of living and investments can be unstable. Or, though your basic planning escaped the economic havoc, you find yourself at age 70 guardian of your grandchildren, or your trip to Mongolia was an absolute blast, but you ended with a broken leg when you fell off a camel, and you now have physical therapy bills piling up. Planning means imagining contingencies.

Your Nest Egg

The money you set aside for retirement is yours to keep or lose, depending on the kinds of investment strategies you follow. *Looking at the retirement savings plans you have is part of the estate inventory you will find in Chapter 10.* However, some basic knowledge about what retirement resources people often have is a good place to begin. You might decide you need to make some changes or want to add a newly available method of saving.

You probably already know the basic parameters of your retirement plan if it is provided through your employment; the human resources department at your company might have mandated a meeting every time a policy change was implemented and plan descriptions and reports are periodically distributed. However, what this information means within the context of estate planning is different than simply deciding how much money to take out of your paycheck every week.

Different companies offer different kinds of retirement plan options, and these have changed dramatically over time. Beyond the ever-shifting laws regarding what gets taxed and what does not, many companies have scaled back their participation in retirement plans — or even the offering of the benefit at all. Once offered as a virtually guaranteed benefit, pension plans and employer contributions to employee retirement accounts are no longer certain.

It is important to know the kind of retirement program in which you participate and the obligations — if there are any — of the entity offering that plan. Professional associations and various government agencies also have retirement plans available, but their plans tend to be a little different from private employers. Once you know what type of plan you have, then you can determine how it fits into your estate plan. It is one of the assets your advisor will need to consider.

Employer pension plans

There are many variations on this theme, so this list will not be exhaustive. It is a place to learn a few things before you go chat with your estate-planning people. Pension and 401(k) plans are the most common ways employers provide a retirement benefit for their employees.

A pension plan is a program set up by an employer, including government agencies, to provide monies to be set aside to pay employees benefits upon retirement. Each employee has an individual account or vested interest, and the employer makes a contribution to each employee's account based on the terms of the plan.

There are two common types of pension plans. One is a defined benefit plan from which the employee will receive a specified amount of money upon retirement; the amount of the disbursement made is based on the number of years of employment. The second is a defined contribution plan, which sets a specific amount — a set percentage of your income — the employee will put into the plan and makes payments only for the amount of money an employee has contributed to the plan. Some of these plans include an employer match.

A qualified pension plan means the amount of money that the employer puts into an employee's account is not taxed as income during the fiscal year the contribution is made. That means the income is tax-deferred — the taxes on that money are paid when it is received by the employee in the form of a monthly pension payment. Employee contributions to these accounts are made on a pre-tax basis as well.

The following conditions might exist:

- **Cost-of-living adjustment**: Some plans will have a variable that will allow for annual increases in the payments made to the employee to help cover the cost of rising prices. Not all plans have this feature.

- **Joint-with-survivor pension**: When an employee dies, her benefits will be paid to her spouse for the remainder of his life. If your spouse waives that right, then the employee's pension payments will be larger — no requirement to set aside extra money for future payments to a spouse — and the pension payments end when the employee dies.

- **Survivor benefit**: A portion of the deceased employee's pension will be paid to the surviving spouse on the employee's death. The amount, frequently a percentage, is set by the terms of the pension plan rules.

- **Waiver**: A written statement declining the right to receive benefits, signed by a spouse. This waiver must be signed to legally sever the right to claim any benefits. An alternative separate agreement, such as a prenuptial agreement, will not be sufficient to create a waiver.

- **Limits**: There can be maximum annual payouts on some pension plans.

There are ways a company can avoid putting cash into a retirement fund, and that is through distributing profits or shares of the company's stock. With a profit-sharing plan, employees receive a portion of the profits earned by the company; the plan determines the amount that will be contributed to each employee's account. The funds can also be used to invest in programs for components such as a disability or medical plan.

Stock bonus plans are established by an employer to give shares of a company's stock to employees. When the employee receives the shares, he must pay taxes based on the value of the stock. An ESOP is a kind of stock bonus plan. The employer contributes shares of its stock to a qualified trust, and the employee only pays taxes based on distributions they receive.

Before an employee can receive any distributions or take full ownership of a pension plan account, the employee has to be vested, meaning that he or she meets the predetermined requirements prescribed by the plan, based on a stated number of years he or she has worked for the employer.

Many employers set up a scale of vested ownership based on the number of years served. For example, if you only work for the company for two years, you are not vested at all, but when you reach three years, you become 15 percent vested. That means you can take ownership of 15 percent of the company's contribution to your pension plan, plus whatever funds you have contributed yourself. Over time, the percentage of your vested ownership increases, and at any point beyond the 0 percent mark, you will be able to take your contributions and whatever vested percentage you have achieved.

More common today is the 401(k) plan — the equivalent of this plan for not-for-profit entities is the 403(b) plan. Named after the IRS code number defining this kind of plan, the 401(k) allows your contributions to be made automatically by your employer via deductions from your paycheck. The advantage is that the money is taken out before taxes, so the amount you pay in taxes now is reduced. You will still have to pay taxes on that money and the interest it earns until you withdraw money from the account. The employer can make a matching tax-deferred contribution to your account. You can take the funds with you when you leave an employer, but the funds must be invested into another approved retirement plan within 60 days, or there will be taxes to pay. This is called rollover. In addition, the percentage of the employer contribution you can take with you will likely depend on the vesting schedule for that plan.

IRAs and Then Some

A retirement plan option that some companies use can also be used by individuals. An annuity is an investment that you create by contributing a specific amount of money over a pre-determined period of time, with a fixed rate of return for a number of years. The money you put into an annuity is not tax-deductible, or taken pre-tax from your paycheck, if it is an employer-sponsored plan. There will be a distribution made to the annuity beneficiary for a fixed term — a specific number of years. The distributions will begin at a pre-determined date — typically the year you retire, so that you will be in a lower income tax bracket — and the distributions will be subject to income tax. The interest on the annuity is accumulated tax-free but will be taxed upon distribution. Here is an example:

In 2008, Rob purchases an annuity from an insurance company for $60,000. The terms of the agreement stipulate that Rob will fund the annuity with ten annual premium payments of $6,000. For ten years, starting in 2018, Rob will receive $9,000 a year from the annuity. The idea is that in 2018, Rob will retire, and his tax bracket will be lower than when he was working full-time. Therefore, he will pay lower taxes on that deferred money.

Those annual payments Rob will receive beginning in 2018 will include the income he earned from the annual premiums he paid, which accumulated tax-free while the annuity was being funded. The only taxable portion of each $9,000 annuity payment Rob gets will be $3,000, because $6,000 of that came from the premium payments he made to fund the annuity. So, for a $60,000 investment, the final value of the annuity will be $90,000.

The return on this investment is low, so it appeals to people who do not feel comfortable with a high-risk investment strategy. A variable annuity is based on the same concept, but the funds are invested in the stock market, so the return depends on how well or poorly the economy does.

If you are self-employed, there is a retirement savings plan for you as well. The Keogh plan — pronounced "key-oh" — is a qualified retirement plan for sole proprietors and partners, but it can also be used by your employees. The restrictions, distributions, and other details are similar to a defined-contribution plan or defined-benefit plan.

An individual retirement arrangement (IRA) is just what it sounds like: a retirement account you set up for yourself. There is a limit to the contributions you can make annually. There is a tax deduction for making these contributions every year, so technically they are tax-free contributions. The taxes come after you withdraw the money, at a time when you are in all probability earning less money, so the amount you pay will be lower — which is one of the main selling points for this kind of retirement investment. You can hold onto these funds until the age of 70 and a half, but after that, the payments will begin.

The next generation of the IRA is called the Roth IRA. Named after its primary legislative sponsor, Senator William Roth from Delaware, contributions to this IRA are also tax-deductible in the year they are made, and taxes are paid when the money is withdrawn. The difference here is that the interest earned while the money is invested will be tax-free if you own the Roth IRA for at least five years. There are limitations on how you can invest the money in your Roth account, and there are big penalties if you take the money out before five and a half years have elapsed, but you can begin distributions that early if you meet the conditions. This IRA also has a distribution requirement that kicks in at age 70 and a half.

Your Government Nest Egg

Social security, Medicare, Medicaid: Most people have heard the terms and been told this is a safety net for those who have absolutely no other resources on which to rely when they are no longer able to work or are legally entitled to receive government benefits. That regular Federal Insurance Contributions Act (FICA) deduction, painfully visible on every paystub you have ever received, is what makes up these government benefits.

The Social Security Administration now sends out annual reports breaking down your contributions and an estimated payment that you are likely to receive. If you are not getting one, you can go to **www.ssa.gov** and review your account. Even if you have not yet seen one of those statements, it is a safe assumption that it will not be enough to pay all your bills when you retire. It is still important to have some understanding of how much of your money the government will give back to you and how it will affect your taxes, and also the taxes your beneficiaries will pay.

Social security retirement benefits

The retirement income provided by social security, commonly referred to as an old-age benefit, depends on how many years you worked full time and paid into the system. If you meet the minimums — ten years of employment or 40 quarter-years — then you are considered to be fully insured. Those who have less than the minimum time in — younger people or those who have worked only sporadically over a long period of time — are called currently insured and are entitled to disability benefits only, if qualified for them.

You can begin receiving social security payments at the age of 62 and 65 — or 67, if you were born after 1960. If you decide to work while receiving benefits, the amount you receive can be reduced. There is an earning limit for various age ranges. However, if you defer receiving your old-age benefit until later in your life, say age 69 or 70, your payments will increase. Electing benefits early at age 62 sets them at a lower rate.

Your social security payments do not have to be paid directly to you. You can designate a beneficiary for the full benefit or split it between you and another person. One-half of your payment can go to your current spouse, or you can designate an ex-spouse to whom you were married for at least ten years who has not remarried. Children can also receive half the payment while you are alive or 75 percent of the payment after you die; adopted children qualify, and under some circumstances, a stepchild might also qualify. Grandchildren and widows or widowers can also receive benefits as long as they meet specific criteria.

Part of this old-age benefit is a lump-sum payment to the surviving spouse or child of the deceased to help with funeral expenses.

Social security disability benefit

If you are unable to work and you qualify as disabled — there is a list of disabilities that, according to the government definition of the word, qualifies or disqualifies you — then you can receive social security disability payments until you reach the age of 65. At that point, you begin to receive the social security retirement benefit at the same rate. The amount of money you receive depends on your work history, so there is no hard-and-fast number for this benefit. You can find more information at **www.ssa.gov/disability**.

Social security supplemental security income (SSI)

SSI is for people who have very little (if any) property, or are blind or disabled in some other way. This is an absolute last-resort situation; it is good to know it is there if you need it, but doing everything possible to avoid that need is an excellent idea.

Medicare and Medicaid

These terms are not interchangeable, even though they both are a medical benefit. Medicare is a medical insurance program offered by the federal government to people who are 65 or older, certain disabled people under the age of 65, and anyone with permanent kidney failure. This last one was added in 1972 out of a concern that people needing life-sustaining dialysis might not be able to afford it. Part A of this coverage is hospital insurance, and Part B is medical insurance. Part B now comes with a monthly premium.

Medicaid is a state-run medical plan that is supported by federal funding and provides minimal medical benefits for the financially needy. To qualify for this plan, you can only possess a set dollar amount in property — $2,022 is a common limit (as of 2010), but different states set different caps for single and married people and other categories such as elderly, pregnant, and disabled. For the state of New York, beginning January 1, 2010, there is no asset or income cap for elibility for Medicaid and related benefits for many classifications of adults. Those who are not eligible for Medicaid due to income or resources might still be able to qualify for New York's Family Health Plus, a public health insurance program for adults aged 18 to 64. Information about New York's system is available from the New York State Department of Health.

Because medical bills can be extremely high, it is entirely possible that a serious illness could devastate your savings and make it necessary to take advantage of this program, so it is important to be aware that it is available if needed.

Protecting Your Eggs

Estate planning is about protecting your property, and that includes the nest eggs and the baskets that hold them. In addition to estimating what money you will be spending from your retirement accounts, you need to consider what might or might not be left in those accounts after you die. You need to do some additional research — with your experts' assistance — to make sure what you expect will be there.

Is your pension plan insured?

The Pension Benefit Guarantee Corporation (PBGC) is a federal agency that can insure and therefore protect some or all of your pension, if your plan qualifies for the coverage and your company purchases the insurance. Not all pensions are insured and, if they are, it might only be for a percentage of each account. You should contact your employer's human resources office to find out more information on whether your pension is insured and, if so, at what level.

Lump sum payments

Be wary of any retirement investment that offers a lump-sum payment over annual distributions. This kind of plan assumes the company will be in business and have the necessary funds when you retire. However, given the way formerly "indestructible" investment institutions and financial companies are failing, there is no guarantee. On the other hand, where lump sum distribution is an option for you to elect, it might be worth considering if the future stability of the plan is in question for any reason. You might be able to roll it over into a personal account or a trust.

Company stock contributions

If your company matches your retirement investments with their own stock, it is a good idea to diversify your holdings as much as possible. If selling your company stock is an option, most likely after you are fully vested, then consider doing that. Company loyalty is one thing; risking your financial security on any one company is a dangerous investment strategy — think WorldCom, Enron, and Bear Stearns. It is not about your commitment to your employer, but your responsibility for your own future. When selling your own company's stock, however, be careful about insider trading rules. Get expert legal advice before committing to these transactions.

Medicare supplemental insurance

Medicare is a wonderful benefit, but it is not perfect. There could be times when Medicare will not pay for some treatments, medications, or doctors you need. If you have health issues, it might be a good idea to investigate and invest in Medigap insurance — an insurance plan specifically designed to pay for Medicare exclusions.

Beneficiaries and their taxes

Always name beneficiaries for any retirement resources you have. If you do not name a beneficiary and a substitute, then the money in those accounts will be added to your probate estate and be subject to the claims of creditors and taxation by state and federal governments. Also, make sure that your beneficiaries know they have been named and what the tax implications might be if they receive those funds. You might decide to make sure your estate provides them with enough money to cover the taxes. *This was discussed further in Chapter 4.*

Retirement/Estate-Planning Strategy

Now that you have an idea of the breadth and scope of retirement savings plans and the resources available to you through the U.S. government, you need to decide how you want to use or save that retirement money.

You can decide to spend it all. You might want to completely exhaust all your retirement funds — after all, that might be why you saved all that money. That way, you do not have to worry about paying the bills when you want to stick your toes in the sand. Your remaining property is your back-up plan. Whatever is left when you die is what you leave to others.

Then there is the frugal approach — choosing to link your retirement needs and spending with your estate planning so that you estimate what you will need until you die, then adding a cushion to preserve the bulk of your estate for your spouse, children, grandchildren, and others.

By using this last approach, you take into account tax payments and future security for the people and organizations that mean the most to you. This is much more work and adds other considerations, such as inflation and keeping up with tax laws. But it is your money, and if you want to have a say in what happens to it when you no longer have a voice, then this is the best way to do that.

CASE STUDY: RETIREMENT ACCOUNTS AND ESTATE PLANNING

Howard McEwen, CFA
Makris Financial Group, Inc.

How much of an impact does a retirement account make on an overall estate plan?

It is important to remember that a will does not dictate the beneficiary of retirement plans such as 401(k)s and IRAs.

The owner of each of those types of plans is allowed to designate a beneficiary. How the beneficiaries are treated is laid down by the 401(k) or IRA's custodial agreement. This custodial agreement overrides anything a will has to say.

Owners should do and look for the following:

- Make sure they designate a primary beneficiary — who gets the money when you die.
- Make sure they designate a contingent beneficiary — who gets the money if you die and your primary beneficiary is also dead.
- Make sure that the custodial agreement allows a per stirpes designation. "Per stirpes" means that if one beneficiary dies, that beneficiary's heirs will be entitled to those assets.
- If needed, make sure beneficiary restrictions can be put in place. If someone is young or has special needs, getting a large chunk of money at your death might not be the best thing for them.
- Regularly review beneficiaries and make sure you have records of who they are — and let your heirs know where those records can be found.

Any negative impact on estate planning is not tremendous if the retirement accounts are managed properly. The primary thing is to keep beneficiary designations up-to-date.

For example, take my client Johnny Jones, who came to my office several years ago. Johnny is a widower in his late 70s. He had a daughter and two sons. His daughter, Irene, was married with two children. His eldest son Max, was married with three children. Bob, the baby of the family, never married and had no children. Bob also had some brushes with the law and is still wrestling with addiction problems.

Johnny retired from a large Fortune 500 company after 30+ years of work. His main asset was his 401(k) plan that he rolled over into an IRA when he retired. Johnny did not give much consideration to designating a beneficiary. In fact, he did not remember discussing it with his advisor.

After growing dissatisfied with his old advisor, Johnny came to my firm. Unfortunately, his eldest son, Max, had died in an industrial accident three years previously. I noticed on his current statements that Max was still listed as a beneficiary.

"Yeah, I just hadn't gotten to that yet," said Johnny.

After looking over the custodial agreement, I explained what would happen to Johnny's money if he happened to die without updating it.

"The custodial agreement doesn't provide a per stirpes provision," I told him. "What this means is that if you die right now, only Irene and Bob will get any money. Max's kids will be totally disinherited."

"You mean, even though he's still on there, his share won't pass on to his kids?"

"Right," I said. "If Irene and Bob decided to disclaim a portion (basically say, 'I don't want Dad's IRA'), Max's kids might inherit — if the courts decide that way. But there are no guarantees that Irene and Bob or the courts will carry out your wishes in this case."

"Also, how will inheriting a large sum of money affect Bob? He's already dealing with addiction issues. Could getting this inheritance actually kill him?"

These are blunt questions with a simple answer: Keep an updated beneficiary designation form, designate those beneficiaries per stirpes, and restrict what kind of money Bob would inherit.

Is there anything a person can do to maximize their retirement plans?

I consider two ways to maximize a client's retirement plan. First is pre-death, by properly allocating a client's account with regard to their risk-reward profile. The second is post-death.

Here is how: In the custodial agreement of the IRA or 401(k), they should verify that their beneficiaries can perform a stretch IRA.

For the majority of Americans, an IRA or 401(k) is their largest asset. By stretching that IRA across multiple generations, an IRA owner can create tremendous wealth for future generations of his family.

How do you stretch an IRA? Simple: by withdrawing the absolute minimum necessary to meet IRS regulations. The funds that remain in the IRA are allowed to compound tax-deferred over a number of years.

Here is a simple example:

David Johansen is married to Patty. They have one son, Sami. Sami has a daughter — Chrissie, age 1, the apple of her grandparents' eye.

Sami is financially self-sufficient, so David designates Chrissie as the sole primary beneficiary on one of his IRAs that Patty will not need if he should die.

In the year David turned 70 and a half, the IRS mandates that he withdraw a percentage of his IRA. This is so they can take it. In that first year, the withdrawal is 3.65 percent.

David takes this withdrawal and then dies.

Chrissie becomes the owner of that IRA, now worth $100,000. Because it was her grandfather's IRA, she is still required to make withdrawals, but those withdrawals are based on her age — not her grandfather's.

Thus, that first year, 1-year-old Chrissie would have to withdraw $1,225. The IRS tables provide a life expectancy of 81.6 years for Chrissie, so $100,000 / 81.6 years = $1,225. If the IRA earns an average of 8 percent over Chrissie's life expectancy, her grandfather's IRA would have paid her $8,167,629.

CHAPTER 9

Setting Priorities

E state planning is more than just deciding what to do with your stuff after your death. Some thought needs to go into what you want to do and how you want to try to prepare for the things you can and cannot predict. A crystal ball to look into the future is wishful thinking, but an even better resource is close at hand — the past. By making time to review the decisions and choices you have already made in your life, you will be able to see what has been important to you.

When you had an opportunity to invest in your 401(k) at work, did you put in the maximum amount allowable or a modest percentage of your income — or did you defer investing until later? Are you glad you made the choice you did, or would you do things differently based on what you know now?

The answers you come up with are an example of how to begin making some decisions. By looking at what you used to think about financial matters, the change in the mix of people in your life, and the organizations you used to support in order to compare that against your present situation, you will be able to see patterns or inconsistencies that are important to the priorities you set for your estate.

This review also needs to include your current financial situation. The credit card debt you do or do not have is influenced by your view of the use of credit. If you do not have any credit cards, that says something about your views on the use of plastic for making purchases and whether paying interest on a purchase is acceptable. Maybe you have a small balance because in the same month you had replaced the tires on your car, the bottom of the water heater decided to drop out, and you simply did not have the cash to pay for a new one. Paying off that balance right away or letting it ride for a bit until you get back from your next business trip also says something

It can be fun to reminisce about the unexpected adventure to South America with a college course you only took because of that cute guy or girl you thought you wanted to date. It can also be difficult, even painful, to remember a family beach vacation that ended up with Grandpa in the hospital and dying three months later. But if you make the effort, you might be able to recall how much fun he had preparing for and involving you and the other kids in the crab boil at sunset, and that will inspire a desire to share that experience with your grandchildren.

The essential part of this process is being attentive to the insignificant, the significant, and everything in between. All these details can serve as helpful pointers now and potential visions for the future.

Your Own Who's Who

Even though every person in your life might not end up in your will, considering the people who are important to you, and those who are not, is one way to identify what matters most to you. Because you are considering your priorities for yourself in addition to your family, friends, and maybe even professional associates, a review of people connected to those priorities makes sense.

The most obvious important people are your family and closest friends. Most people can rattle off the names of people they are related to by birth, marriage, or mutual agreement — friends frequently become "chosen family." A bit more thought might be needed when considering extended family or distant relatives.

It might be a given that family is so important to you that everyone living in your house will sit down to eat at least one meal together every day, often dinner; kids home from college or the grandparents visiting from out of state for a week all know this is expected. It might also be known by your children that there are some family members they never see but for whom everyone signs the family holiday card each year; if those same people send a note with a small gift for a birthday or graduation, a thank-you note will be written, because those distant relatives are equally important. These relatives are always invited to parties even though they never come.

Priorities revealed:

- Time with family is more than important; it is essential.

- Every celebration that calls for a party begins with a call to family members to find out what dates work for them.

- Even though some relatives live far away or might even be reclusive, you make sure your children keep in touch; you want them to have a strong sense of family regardless of proximity.

Implications for estate planning:

- Immediate family is so important that you want to make sure they have what they need.

- A desire to leave something to every family member, be it cash or a memento.

- Is everyone clear about how important your family is to you? Just because family time and ties are important to you does not mean your siblings, children, or anyone else will be aware of this. Clearly communicating this priority to your family is a good idea so that when the will is read and the distant relatives are included, your wishes are carried out, and the immediate family does not contest your bequests.

People come and go from our lives at various times for different reasons. The people with whom you surround yourself now are probably a quite different mix when you consider the people from your past. Even though life circumstances play a part in that coming and going of people, the effort you make to include, or exclude, people from your life places a value on that relationship. If you go out of your way to call someone or delete a message from the answering machine with no intention of calling the person back, it says something about how you feel about that individual.

Looking at the changes in your personal circle is one way to approach this review of people. For example: After being widowed, you might have lost touch with your in-laws; this does not bother you because they never liked you or the fact that you married their son or daughter. The kids are old enough to go visit their grandparents when they want to.

You remarried and have become close to the extended family of your current husband or wife. This new, blended family includes an alcoholic uncle you simply cannot stand to be around, even though everyone thinks he is the life of every party. Similarly, when your kids get married, they do not want to have to juggle multiple Thanksgiving dinners because they embrace the blended family as positive and open. So, they propose a huge family gathering of all sides that results in meeting new family members with whom you now enjoy weekend camping trips and a weekly bowling league.

Priorities revealed:

- You want to have people in your life with whom you can have a friendly, healthy relationship.

- You are willing to meet familial obligations, such as making an effort with your in-laws when your wife was alive, but once an obligation is fulfilled, you are all right with letting it go.

- Distancing yourself from people who can be harmful to you or your family is also all right, but you try to do it in a manner that does not upset others.

- Family is important but not exclusive; "biological family-only" events rarely happen because they feel exclusionary.

Implications for estate planning:

- Including people who are not related by blood in your will must be handled legally and carefully to avoid any contest after you are gone. State laws governing family inheritance are clear; the same cannot be said for non-relatives.

- Leaving money to a family member with an addiction or some other life problem — maybe an abusive spouse or unscrupulous children — might require the use of a trust and a trustee to avoid the potential disasters that can result.

- Give some consideration to not including someone in your will. Giving a significant bequest to a specific person might not sit well with you, but a small gift could be considered to avoid a contest due to complete exclusion.

The faces of people you call friends can also change over time. For example: Debbie, a friend from grade school with whom you kept in touch via letters when you lived in different states is now a neighbor, thanks to her job transfer. The college roommate with whom you shared many late-night study sessions and much burnt microwave popcorn moved from experimenting with drugs to hardcore use. The last time he called you to bail him out of jail, you told him it was the last time, and you have not heard from him since.

Then there are the people we encounter just doing our everyday business. We can easily take them for granted, not realizing their importance until something happens. For example, there is Betty, the elderly woman who lives down the street and has no family. She ends up in a nursing home after breaking her hip, ending your Friday morning tea-and-cookies visits. There is the librarian who knows you by name and suggests books you might like. And there is the mechanic who normally changes the oil in your car, but one day is not there when you stop in. His son is at the register and explains that he was feeling tired and needed a few days off.

Priorities revealed:

- Your awareness of and concern for others extends beyond your immediate circle to acquaintances.

- Frequenting local shops and businesses is important to you; you go out of your way to avoid impersonal, big-box stores.

- You prefer to be a part of the community in which you live.

- Neighbors matter.

Implications for estate planning:

- Continuing to support the organizations and institutions you appreciate and that have been a source of friendships for you, such as your local library, when you are no longer around to cast your vote for a levy or make a donation might be added to your list of bequests.

- The support you give to a family-owned business might not be significant, but something in your estate might be helpful to them: Your mechanic might appreciate the tools you use for fixing your car.

- Donating your book collection to the local library would make your family happy; they are not big readers, and it would be one less thing to handle when it comes time to sell the house.

By taking time to consider people, you will naturally think of memories and specific milestones in life that are related. The things you experience directly or simply witness also provide an opportunity to review your priorities.

Memory Lane

Looking back to the mundane as well as the amazing through the filter of estate planning makes it possible to see how the past can inform and even direct the future. If you see accumulated knowledge and financial resources as the means to adding some adventure and comfort to the later years in your life, not just gifts for others, then you can live unfulfilled dreams or expand on some wonderful experiences.

Consider that trip to South America: Would you have begged, borrowed, or gone into debt to have the extra month in the rainforest, knowing you might never have the chance to go back? Look at this year's vacation plan. Are you going anywhere near a rainforest? Would you consider changing your plans to return to that place south of the border? Are you disappointed that you cannot change your plans? Would you like to go again if you could come up with the money for the trip? Or has the idea of some tropical disease soured you on that kind of adventure? Does a cruise ship that anchors off the coast and includes a one-day trip to the very edges of the greenery sound more like your idea of fun?

There are any number of events from the past that underscore the priorities you had at that time and how far you have drifted into another view of what is important. Here are a few memory joggers to get you thinking:

Family time:

- Vacations with immediate family only/large, extended gatherings.

- Annual visit from the cousins was fun/torture.

- Having a sleepover at a friend's house made you want to stay there / go home.

- Thanksgiving dinner did/did not include a "kids' table."

- How many parties were held at your house, and which ones did you enjoy or loathe?

School:

- Favorite subject/class.

- Memorable teacher — the one who got you excited about learning and how he or she did that.

- The class bully and how you handled him or her when it was your turn to be picked on.

- Public or private? Liked or disliked? Why?

- Science fairs — participation by choice or force, and the level of desire to hide under your display table during judging.

- Fraternity/sorority/independent thinker?

- Class office positions held by election or appointment.

Extracurricular:

- Scouting, or made fun of Scouts?

- Reporter for the school paper.

- Band.

- Helped teachers clean after school.

- Clubs.

- Sports.

Do-overs:

- Your first/second/third marriage.

- Rehabbing the cute bungalow that ended up selling for less than you paid.

- Studying economics and only taking one art class in college.

- Giving up your film cameras for digital.

- Donating your turntable and all your jazz record albums.

- Not touring Europe before having kids.

These life experiences are more than just a reflection of how you used to feel or what you were forced into doing by your parents. Your recollections and the way you respond to them now are a measure of what matters to you now.

Maybe that beach house you rented in 1998 is exactly the kind of home you wanted to have when you dreamed of living in a beach house. Perhaps that dream is never going to come true, given the circumstances of your life, but there is still time to make changes right now. You have eight more years until you are fully vested in your pension fund, so you have eight years to plan. Prepare to sell your existing home in the suburbs; help your kids deal with the shock of your move to Nags Head, North Carolina; and get your finances in order. Your accountant and lawyer can get to work on the papers for the living trust you need to make sure your retirement years will be non-stop beach time.

If having fun in your life was something you passed up to fulfill obligations or deferred to achieve other goals, then you might decide recreation is so critical that you want to share that lesson with your grandkids. One way to do that is to make sure they have the "mad money" necessary to fund the fun: Set up a "mad money" trust for each grandchild to do whatever they want in the summer between high school and college. Once you make that a priority — because their parents have already funded their tuition and other fees — you can figure out how much you need to save or how much you need to not spend from your retirement account to fund those trusts.

Reminiscing often includes groups of people with like-minded views and dreams. Those groups also matter when it comes to estate planning.

Your "People"

Not everyone has an entourage of groupies, support staff, and employees to do their bidding. More often, you are the one doing the work, and frequently it is for a non-profit organization. Your priorities about which causes or institutions to support have most likely changed over the years. The arts, once a luxury on a limited budget, are now at the top of your annual giving list, but the Peace Center that was struggling to survive in the basement of the dilapidated building next to your first apartment has moved to the storefront and still gets 20 hours of your time every month.

The institutions that rely on your time, money, or donations of office supplies have captured your imagination or hopes, or maybe just inspired you with their underdog determination. Whatever the reason, they are important to you. While they consider you among their supporters, i.e., their people, the fact is that your desire to see them succeed makes them your people.

Considering the non-profits you have supported at different times in your life might spark an interest to get involved or lend support again. Life changes; a parent dying of cancer might inspire you to add the American Cancer Society or a hospice to the list of charities you wish to support.

Because estate planning is more than distributing belongings after you die, the importance you place on these groups needs to be factored into your priorities. Maybe the Peace Center is on the verge of needing to move because they are growing so rapidly. Or perhaps that old bakery building you bought a few years ago has not turned out to be the successful investment property your real estate agent swore it would be; putting it into a charitable trust or making an outright donation of it to the Peace Center might be the best way to help them and reduce the amount of real property in your estate.

If you do move to that beach house in Nags Head, the time you spend at the cat rescue shelter is no longer going to be an option. You know they desperately need volunteers, but even more desperate is a need for cat food. A donation of cash for the purchase of food is only going to be possible if you set up a way to make it happen.

After you fund the mad-money trusts, make sure you have enough to live on during retirement and cover the cost of your disability insurance as the safety net; it might be that you only have enough in your estate to support two charities. Which will they be — the arts organizations, the Peace Center, or the cat shelter? Do you want to set aside a little extra in case you find some institution in Nags Head that you might want to support later?

These are the difficult decisions that must be made if you prefer not to work extra hours or cut into your current spending to allow for future expenditures.

Must-Do

The things you never thought you would get to do in this lifetime or the envious moments spent listening to others describe what you have always dreamed about doing inspires some people to create a must-do list. Be it mountain climbing or scuba diving, going out to dinner at a five-star restaurant, or taking two weeks off work to just stay at home and relax, the things you feel are important enough to put on a list are important enough to make happen.

Setting priorities for your estate planning is a means to that "must-do" end. Identifying what matters most right now and what you thought was important but now realize is no big thing makes it possible to consider financial decisions that will have an impact now and later.

```
CASE STUDY: A FINANCE
COACH FOR ESTATE PLANNING
Sue Holm, Founder
Make Peace with Money
```

How should a person make decisions about his or her priorities?

All major decisions about financial priorities should be made with a trusted advisor or counselor. For some folks, that can be family or friends. For some, that is a financial planner or advisor. If someone has emotional issues about money, a financial counselor, coach, or therapist who is comfortable with money issues should be consulted.

There is an element of spirituality that also touches these decisions during life and when contemplating death. How much to give away? To whom? Why? When? Charitable giving, tithing (donating a fixed percentage of income to a religious institution), and giving back are all rich issues for discussion — among families, faith communities, and in our world. Does charity begin at home? What does that mean? What does that look like? Is money good, bad, or neutral? Are money and spirituality linked or not?

How do people apply those priorities to their decisions about disbursing their money and property after their death?

By not planning, people allow the state to dictate the disposition of their money and property. For those who have priorities, familial or spiritual, those priorities will drive the nature of the disbursal.

Why do people fight over things like a toaster or a chair after someone has died?

Because they have unresolved emotional issues, either about themselves and their self-worth, or their relationship with the deceased.

How can the person who owns the toaster or chair prepare his or her family for that situation?

If people are clear about their intentions in creating estate plans and have the occasion to discuss their intent with their family, it can defuse some of the tension. The person who owns things can create an atmosphere in which it is OK to ask for what you want while they are still alive. They can ask their loved ones what they need or want as a remembrance. They can create a system to disbursing things not otherwise specified in the will.

How often should those priorities be revisited?

Financial priorities should be revisited at all major life milestones — marriage, divorce, birth of children, the children achieving their majority (turning 18), birth of grandchildren.

What are the benefits of working with a financial counselor or coach?

The benefits include financial clarity, mastery, and ultimately peace with money. This manifests in decreased debt, increased saving, and earning what you are worth.

Many people do not know that financial counseling or coaching is available. Many people with financial issues know they need help; they just do not know how to find it. Many people think that because they are smart and successful in most areas of their life, they should know what to do with money, or that they will be able to figure it out themselves. This can be increasingly frightening and frustrating as they try and fail on their own.

Among the most productive discussions between a financial counselor and client are those that involve the differentiation between needs and wants and how to prioritize them.

How should a financial professional collaborate with other people in an estate-planning team?

Ideally, during the financial counseling process, the counselor will refer the client to an estate-planning professional if the client does not yet have an estate plan.

Financial counselors can be an excellent resource for estate-planning professionals working with surviving spouses or partners who need or want some structure and support while they assume financial responsibility for themselves or for the estate.

Additionally, estate-planning professionals should consider referring clients who inherit sums of money or assets they are inexperienced in managing to a financial counselor.

How does a person go about choosing a financial professional? What characteristics/experience should a client look for?

As this is not a licensed or regulated field, it is important that clients examine the credentials of anyone they are considering as a financial counselor or coach. Training agencies, such as the Financial Recovery Institute (**www.financialrecovery.com**), frequently list those counselors or coaches who have been trained and certified.

Many clients seeking financial counseling have not talked about their money issues with anyone. They frequently have conscious and subconscious money secrets. It is imperative that clients trust their financial counselor, and that a financial counselor or coach be able to deal with the client's emotional issues that underlie the money issues.

CHAPTER 10

Choosing Who, What, How, When and Why

N ow that you know what you own or need to save, and have an idea of what you will need to keep for yourself as you go forward as well as a sense of the people and organizations you would like to support with your hard-earned assets, it is time to put all that information together into a comprehensive estate plan. The detailed overview of the choices you have for delivering assets provided in Chapters 5-8 is just that — an overview. The legal restrictions and limitations of different kinds of trusts, annuities, insurance policies, and other financial vehicles will help you identify potential resources that will meet your goals. Only professionals in estate planning are going to be able to make your estate plan meet your goals and be legally binding.

Beyond the difficult choices of who gets what, you also need to choose the CPAs, lawyers, financial advisors, insurance agents, and others who will be a part of your estate-planning and management team. Many of these people receive commissions for the "sale" of different kinds of products. The trust that might be best for you could have a smaller commission than the trust with plenty of extras — a planner who is doing his or her job will suggest what is best for your needs, not his or her checking account. Even though a less expensive firm might be attractive while you are still building up your estate, consider the longevity of the firm; there is the distinct possibility that later you will have a larger estate if you get proper guidance.

Something with such a long-term impact as your estate planning deserves a high level of care, thoughtfulness, and attention.

Who and When: The Matching Game

The solitaire game Concentration, referred to as "the matching game" by many preschoolers, involves placing all the cards in a deck upside down on a table in a grid pattern. Each player turns over two cards; if they do not match, then they are flipped back over, and the next player takes a turn. The goal is to keep flipping over cards and remembering where each one is so that you can make matches — two fours, two queens, two eights — until all matches are made; the person with the most sets of matches wins. It is a good way to teach children how to increase their concentration skills, but the premise of the game is also a good method for distributing your estate. The key difference is that you decide what makes a match.

If you are unsure of how to begin, consider the sticky-note method. Put the name of each person and institution you wish to support with your estate; include yourself in that list if you plan on creating a living trust or dedicating other resources to your retirement that will be a part of your estate plan. In the case of multiple beneficiaries — you benefit from a living trust during your life and there is a beneficiary for that trust after your death — be sure to note both people.

Make a sticky note for each asset that you listed on the *Your Estate in Black and White* worksheet found in Appendix A of this book.

Now get the *Prioritization* worksheet found in Appendix A of this book so you can compare what you think you want against the practical structure of the estate you are crafting.

Then lay them all out by matching them up, and see whether the matches are what you want them to be.

This method gives you the chance to see the differences in the amounts, property, and other bequests you make. That side-by-side comparison might also raise questions in your mind about the implications of the distribution.

Carol tends to be a black-and-white kind of person, so she might get upset when she learns the difference in the value of the property she gets and the Nags Head property going to Danny — the property she gets is worth 50 percent less. The fact that her profession is rehabbing houses and that she can invest a small amount to make the property equal in value — if not more — is something you might want to explain. Or, you might decide to add some fixer-upper cash to her bequest to soften the blow.

You might not feel right about giving Jeanine a $50,000 bequest when Mary Lynn is getting $60,000, even though you know it is what they need. Add a little something to Jeanine's bequest if that makes you feel better.

But then, all these differences might not bother you in the least. You know what you are doing and why, and because it is your estate plan, the issue of fairness is a moot point.

Another thing this exercise can do is provide an opportunity to consider bundling or separating items in your estate as part of a bequest. If you are looking only at the dollar value of a gift, packaging together the sentimental items with stocks, bonds, or cash will give you a chance to customize a bequest to the person who receives it.

Mary Lynn is not a reader, so the book collection would not mean as much to her as Jeanine, who is getting her degree in creative writing.

The charitable trust for the Peace Center that includes the old bakery is an incredibly generous gift — the largest they have ever received. That being said, the actual expense of the upgrades needed to meet building codes will take a big chunk out of their operating budget. The extra $10,000 can be invested until they are ready to do the work, and it is also a way to motivate other donors to kick in some support.

It is not necessary to use sticky notes for this exercise, but it is important to note that a light breeze could blow away your efforts. Imagine how an overly enthusiastic pet can scatter pieces of paper that do not stick. A large dry-erase board or chalkboard serves the same purpose. Regardless of the method, the ultimate goal is simple: Match up your priorities with the people and gifts you wish to give.

Once you have settled on who is getting what, taking a digital photo of your makeshift plan could be helpful later when you decide you want to make changes. *See Chapter 12 for more information on this.* You will have a record of your notes and can use that to reconstruct and revisit this process, or maybe you will want to show it to a financial advisor. Converting this information to an electronic document is a possibility by using a table in a word-processing document or using a spreadsheet program.

An estate plan is something you will need to revisit and change regularly, so consider keeping your notes and other planning documents for a while, at least until you are sure you have all the information saved in some other format.

When: Today, Tomorrow, or Later?

An important strategy for estate planning that goes unused by many is early gifting. The traditional or customary time for distributing an estate is after a person dies, but staying with the traditional can mean a larger estate and more taxes. A gift tax might still apply to the property you hand over early, but, given the rate of tax increase, it is entirely possible this could mean a lower tax bill for the beneficiary.

Another thing to consider is when the beneficiary will get the most benefit from the gift you make. Your estate is yours to dispose of how and when you choose; if you want to take advantage of an opportunity to help a relative or charity in need, then you can factor that into your estate plan.

Jeanine graduated from high school with an International Baccalaureate (IB) degree — a special education program offered by her high school. She has changed her major from creative writing and is now majoring in political science in college. The whole family thinks she is making a bad decision and that she is too young to understand how she will be limiting her career choices to politics only. "Why be a politician? Everyone knows women can only go so far before they hit a glass ceiling," they think.

You see the potential Jeanine sees — and more. International corporations, government embassies, and a long list of opportunities await the person who has the background and understanding of multiple cultures and knows how to navigate the intricacies of governmental policy and social mores.

The cultural club she belongs to is planning a trip to Mongolia, and she desperately wants to go, but her education trust fund will not cover the expenses of the trip. She can legally go on the trip, but she does not have the cash. Because you want to encourage her passion and efforts to get a well-rounded education, not to mention some invaluable experience before graduation, you decide to create an education trust for Jeanine that specifically covers the cost of school-related travel.

Even though Jeanine will not receive any other money from your estate, you can remind yourself that she is getting an immediate benefit that will have long-term implications for her ability to build her own estate. It might be helpful to explain this to her, too.

Choosing to give some gifts early, putting conditions on other gifts, and explaining the logic behind why you are doing these things all need careful consideration. If your family is competitive or has some other characteristics that could inspire resentment or other negative reactions — before or after your death — you might want to consider sharing your reasoning. This can be done in the form of a letter to each family member that will be opened after your death, or at a one-on-one meeting in which you discuss the terms and conditions of your will and estate.

Regardless of how open or confidential you are about your financial matters, remember that after you are gone, your ability to explain yourself is limited. When deciding on the timing of your gifts, keep this in mind.

How: The Professionals

There is a host of people from which to choose your estate-planning team. Who does what and areas of specialty can get confusing. A CPA can address tax issues, but so can a lawyer who specializes in tax law. Which is better will depend on what your needs are. Chapter 2 describes the important people making up your estate-planning team. Please refer to that chapter for a review of the parties.

The best way to determine who can help you with your estate planning is to look at your needs, preferences, and expectations. If the content of this book is the extent of your estate-planning knowledge, then you have much to learn before you can check "estate-planning documents prepared" off your to-do list. A professional with access to multiple resources of current information that is written for the consumer and who has the patience to answer questions will be essential for you. Someone who knows what a QTIP is without looking in the glossary might prefer to seek a professional who can provide more detailed information without getting overly technical.

Beyond that, the circumstances of your life and interests are going to impact the time you have to spend, your level of commitment to achieving whatever timetable you set for completion, and the people with whom you work. Traveling across town for meetings might not be possible if you are going to be caring for your 18-month-old twin nieces while your sister goes back to school for a semester.

Some factors to consider before you begin putting together your estate-planning team are:

- **Interest level**: If a root canal without anesthesia sounds like more fun than estate planning, or you have a true desire to plan but lack the time to make it happen, then you have some sense of how much you do/do not want to engage in this process.

  Consider that 75 percent of the population does not do comprehensive estate planning before they die, but the U.S. and state governments have enough laws on the books to take control of and benefit from your lifetime of work and savings. Focus on the benefits of this hard work, and consider the good things it can accomplish for you and those who matter most to you.

- **Deadlines**: Any significant milestones that are coming up sooner or later.

  If you have a three-month world tour planned for next year, it would be a good idea to get this wrapped up before you leave the country. If you are not going anywhere for the next few years, you can take this at a slower pace.

- **Health issues**: Even if you are healthy right now, your age and family medical history could impact your planning timetable.

  Grandma Nan lived to be 100, but all her sisters died of breast cancer in their 60s, and you are age 24, 48, or 56. Your father-in-law died at the age of 40 of a massive heart attack, and your husband is 48 years old.

- **Family matters**: Collaborative relationships, disagreements, a marriage or birth, long-standing feuds, addiction struggles, helping with child care, and everything in between can impact your decision-making and the time you can commit to this process.

The bickering between two siblings might inspire a desire to cut them both out of your will, while a newly married couple means one more person to add — maybe two, if baby makes three.

- **Charities**: Like families, organizations go through considerable change. Insignificant change, such as a staffing change, or significant change, such as building a new facility, could influence your time commitment to estate planning, in addition to your giving.

The Friends Meeting House where you study received the permits and approvals necessary to go forward with the construction of their new building ahead of schedule; instead of breaking ground in five years, they begin in eight months. You may need to revise when they receive the money you have left them.

Once you have made up your mind to follow through with this estate planning you have been avoiding, and you know what your schedule looks like — as much as anyone can — you need to consider the components and status of your belongings. If you are just beginning to build your estate, such a will requires fewer professionals than someone who has 32 years in the workforce and multiple resources to consider. Special circumstances can complicate the process for any estate of any value.

The following offers an example of the many factors that may come into play when developing your estate family.

Family:

Blended: His, his, hers, hers, and ours
Unconventional: Same sex, interracial
Adoption: Domestic or international

Foreign-born spouse: Not a U.S citizen

Personal:

Career changes
Multiple relocations: Domestic or overseas
Frequent layoffs
Mental health concerns
Felony arrest(s)

Income:

Structured settlements
Rental property
Inheritance
Royalties
Unemployment

Outgoing:

Child support
Alimony
Elder care for parents
Terminal illness

Whether these things affect you or your estate, they need to be taken into consideration. In addition to being information your estate planner will need to know — the firm you approach might not want to deal with estate issues related to people who are not U.S. citizens — they might have implications for your budget.

The adage "You get what you pay for" is a good rule of thumb for the level of risk you take with your estate-planning team members if you make decisions based exclusively on the fees they charge. It is entirely possible that you will get lucky with phone-book roulette and stumble across a CPA who has your best interest at heart; and even though he has considerable experience, he is willing to charge next to nothing for his expertise because he wants you to keep your money. But the high-priced estate-planning firm, with more credentials than you have ever seen, is not necessarily going to give you the kind of service you need or collaborate with your other estate-planning partners.

The process of selecting the professionals with whom you will work requires some scrutiny of individual professional standards — credentials for a CPA, passing the bar exam (or not) — but some general expectations for this group of people can be defined. Consider the following when choosing a professional to assist you with your estate plan:

- Do you recognize the name of the school from which he graduated? What does he do to stay current with changes in financial markets?

- How many years of experience does this person have?

- What is the focus or areas of expertise for that experience and the duration in each area?

- Do they have a private practice, group practice, or corporate environment? Find out whether the expertise of others is readily available if a question or problem arises.

- Ask the Better Business Bureau and allied professional associations — the American Bar Association (ABA) for lawyers — for complaints, reprimands, or any other questionable business practices.

- Ask about the nature of relationships with the providers of the products the individual or firm offers; ask for a disclosure of commissions and other perks provided to the individual professional or firm.

- Review the Web site for current clients. Does the list include people with estates similar to yours, or are they high-worth individuals and business owners? A firm that specializes in businesses might do personal estate planning as an aside for those companies, but that is not its area of expertise.

- Talk to previous and current clients or friends and associates who recommend, or are wary of, the person and/or company.

Once you have a short list of people to interview for your estate-planning team, prepare as much information as possible in advance of your first meeting. This will help you and the professionals you interview to quickly determine how they might, or might not, be able to help you craft your plan.

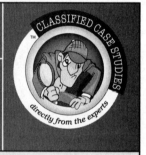

CASE STUDY: ESTATE-PLANNING CHOICES

Scott J. Malof, CPA/PFS
SS&G Financial Services, Inc.
Certified Public Accountants
and Advisers
www.SSandG.com

What information should a person collect to prepare for this process?

When preparing for the estate-planning process, people should begin preparing a snapshot of where they are today. Create a family tree of personal details including ages and health status for immediate family members as well as those whom you might have to care for, such as an aging parent. Also, remember guardian nominations for your minor children, trustee nominations that are part of a will or other estate options, executor nominations to execute your will, separation/divorce agreements, and tax returns for the past couple of years.

This snapshot should include all relevant financial information, including listings of assets and liabilities, details of all insurance policies, and current and future income streams. Your financial situation would include a detailed personal balance sheet listing all assets and liabilities, life insurance policy details, other insurance coverage such as disability coverage, and income and expenses now and in the future. The last piece, and often the most difficult, is your goals and expectations, including legacies.

What are the most overlooked loopholes or opportunities people miss when coordinating the financial aspect of their estate?

Here are a few:

- Not using up each spouse's applicable exclusion amount, both at the federal and state level. For example, you could leave everything to your spouse.
- Assuming the kids can divvy everything up fairly without fighting. This could be a mistake, not an opportunity.
- Not using a gifting plan.

How does the power of gifting affect an estate plan?

Currently, all individuals can give any other individual up to $12,000 annually without using up their lifetime applicable exclusion amount of $2,000,000. To the extent given away, this money is not included in the donor's estate at death.

Let us say a couple has two children, two surviving parents, and four grandchildren. This couple could give away $192,000 annually — eight people times $12,000 in gifts times two donors. If this were done for a period of 20 years, the donors could remove $3.84 million from their estate, excluding the impact of earnings over those years. This could have a taxable federal estate at the highest rate, which is currently 45 percent. This would be a $1,728,000 savings.

The downside to gifting is relinquishing the control over the property. Also, giving large sums of money to minor children does not come without ramifications, both good and bad. This is why estate planning can be so hard for so many people. The answers are not always about saving the most money or passing down the most wealth. It truly comes back to meeting a person's wishes.

How do state laws and federal laws affect estate-planning choices?

Federal and state laws have an enormous impact on estate planning. When people are determining where they would like their property ultimately to go, they need to be cognizant of the legal ramifications of their choices. For example, the rules for the transfer of property in a community-property state vary from those in a common-law state. Knowledge of these rules will help people to plan accordingly.

Also, much of estate planning includes trying to minimize any transfer taxes that may come due. The amount of potential federal and/or state estate or gift tax has an enormous impact on the estate plan. For example, a couple with a $10 million estate could easily save over $1 million with some very simple estate-planning techniques. If this couple implements a gifting plan over a number of years, the savings possibility goes up substantially. Currently, the highest federal estate tax rate is 45 percent, leading to quite a savings when the estate is properly managed.

Confidentiality is very important to many people — sometimes from the general public, but also from other family members. State laws especially govern what information must be made public record through probate or disclosed on a limited basis, such as through trust reporting to beneficiaries. Clients need to determine how much they want the public or their heirs to know about what they have, how they are passing it, and to whom.

CHAPTER 11

Planning Your Estate: Last Will and Testament in New York

As mentioned in our general discussion in this book, specific requirements for drafting valid wills are directed and controlled by the laws of each state. While there are some common principles, not all states are the same. It is always advisable to obtain legal counsel to assist you in drafting your last will and testament, especially if you have more than one residence in different states, or if you draw up your will in a different state than where you live. You should consult an attorney to ensure your will conforms to the proper controlling state law, as it will likely differ in various states. Additionally, state laws change from time to time.

Thus, it is important to understand New York's statutory requirements for valid wills at the time you draft yours. Otherwise, your efforts to bequeath your property could fail; regardless of what you wrote down as your intent to distribute your property according to "your will," it will be the same as if you wrote nothing. You will have died intestate — without a will. In that event, your property will be distributed according to state law, possibly in ways you never imagined, and often at greater court costs.

According to current New York law, if you are a least age 18 and mentally competent with "sound memory" to do so, you can make a will in the state of New York.

Elements of a Valid New York Will

A *holographic* will is a document written either fully in the testator's hand or dated and signed by the testator but not witnessed. Only a handful of states recognize holographic wills. New York will recognize a holographic will only if it was written by a person in active military or maritime service at the time.

Otherwise, to be valid, a will must be written, dated, and signed at the end by the testator and witnessed by at least two disinterested adult witnesses. If the testator is unable to physically sign the will, he or she may direct another person to sign for the testator in the testator's presence, and the person so signing will have to also append his or her name and address and explain that he or she is signing for the testator at such direction. Obviously, in such a circumstance, the presence of the witnesses is much more than just a formality.

Witnesses

A witness who is also a beneficiary of the will in some way is not automatically disqualified as a witness in New York, but that witness *will not be permitted to receive the legacy in the will unless there are also two other disinterested witnesses to the will.*

For this reason, a person who receives a benefit in the will should not also be one of the witnesses who "count" to make it a valid will. There are reasons that a testator might wish to include such a person as an additional witness, such as to ensure that person cannot contest the will exists, or to include the person for a family reason. You are permitted to have more than two witnesses to the will. What is required is that there be two to make the will valid. Also, the two witnesses must sign in the testator's presence within 30 days of the testator's signing of the will. Usually witnessing is done at the same time a will is signed, which is the recommended best practice. Occasionally, though, a person prepares a will without the necessary disinterested witnesses readily available. New York law requires you round up the witnesses within 30 days, acknowledge the document to be your will and that you have signed it, and have the witnesses affix their signatures and date. If you prepare your will with the assistance of legal counsel, as you should, your counsel will ensure that the proper New York formalities are followed to create a valid will.

Witnesses are a legal requirement for wills to be valid. Their necessity is highlighted especially in will contest actions. They could be called upon to testify to the circumstances of the signing of the will, the appearance of the testator as to soundness of mind, or the fact that the testator signed the will him/herself in their presence or affirmed his or signature in their presence.

One lawyer's anecdotal story illustrates the type of shenanigans that take place when it comes to wills. He was called out late at night by a client's son who asked him to come to the house because the client (the mother) was very ill and wanted the lawyer to witness her signing her new will and take it into his custody. "Couldn't this wait until morning?" the lawyer asked. "She insists it has to be you," said the son, "and I'm not sure she will last through the night." The lawyer, having served the client for many years, went to the house and was ushered into the woman's bedroom, where he found her propped on her pillows, a document before her on the bed, and a pen in her hand.

The son said to him, "Mother is having trouble speaking now, but I will help her sign the will, and we can both witness it." Whereupon, the son took the mother's hand and started to guide it upon the paper. "Wait a moment," said the lawyer, and he spoke to his client, who did not answer. He stepped closer and reached for her wrist. The son attempted to interfere, but the lawyer pushed him away and sought a pulse. As you have now guessed, the mother had already passed away, and the son was attempting to get the new will signed posthumously, in hopes the lawyer would either be fooled or go along with it. Truth is stranger than fiction. Of course the son could not have been a valid witness anyway because — as will be discussed further — he was named in the purported will. Whatever the mother might have intended about the new will, she died before signing it, and nor did she create an oral will, as will be further discussed.

Intent or Agreement to Make a Valid Will — An Exception to Witnesses' Signatures

New York law recognizes the concept of a testator's "agreement" to make a will if all the elements of making a will are met except for the actual signing of the witnesses who were present when the testator signed. This is an exceptional case and requires proof through a probate court hearing and final determination of the court. It should not be relied upon to always cure a testator's lack of knowledge or mistake as to properly finalizing the will. For the court to be able to decide there was an "agreement" — or an intent — to make a will, the decedent must have written out the will, or had it prepared and signed it at least, in the presence of witnesses. The person who brings the will to court to be validated must prove it by clear and convincing evidence and, if successful, might be able to collect the cost of fees back from the attorney who assisted in preparing it, if the attorney was at fault in not having it properly attested. These provisions of New York's law underscore the importance of obtaining legal counsel who is certified in estate planning and probate law in the first place.

Changing Your Will — Codicils

You have made your will and it is done. However, along comes something new: Another child is born; new property is acquired or property is sold; a divorce occurs; a marriage happens; a death happens; or a loss occurs. Life changes.

Whatever the reason, you decide you want to change something in your will, just one provision or part of it, or you just want to add something to it without changing the whole thing. A codicil is an addition you can write and attach to or put with your existing will. You may do this in New York by following the same procedures required to make a formal will, with two witnesses, and designating it as a codicil to your will. If there are multiple codicils and they contradict each other, the most recently signed and dated codicil will be the provision that is considered valid.

Oral Will

New York law permits a person to make an oral will, also called a nuncupative will, only during active military or maritime service.

Where to Keep Your Will

Keep your will in a safe place, but one where it can be found when you are no longer here. Many people deposit their will with the attorney who assisted in drafting it. This is not a bad practice, especially if the attorney or his or her firm is the legal fiduciary whom you wish to assist with the probate of your will. You could also keep the will in a home safe that is fireproof or with the person whom you have named as your executor or executrix of the will.

Beneficiaries, Debts, and Entitlements

Subject to certain limitations, you can leave your property and possessions to anyone you wish. If you are married and you disinherit your spouse, though, your spouse has legal rights under New York law to take against the will. If there are no children, a surviving spouse is entitled to 50 percent of the estate. If you have any surviving children, your spouse is entitled to claim one-third of the estate. Your bequests can be proportionately distributed only after the spousal legal entitlement is first satisfied.

If you wish to disinherit one or more of your children, including any not yet born, it is best to expressly say so in the will, even though the words might sound harsh in black and white. Omission by silence might raise a question of mistake and open your intent to dispute. Wills have been challenged successfully by children appearing who were presumed dead, who were not known to exist, who were born after the will was prepared, or who were ostensibly disinherited by simply not being named in it. What the testator intended about these children was not clear; therefore, it was presumed the testator intended to include the child in the estate.

As a result, you are well advised to foresee these circumstances and either expressly state that Junior is not receiving anything under the will, stating a reason, or give a token bequest to Junior, such as $1. In some cases, a child is not included in an inheritance because he or she has already received a share during the testator's lifetime. In others, there are simply bad feelings. Your attorney will advise you on the best way to handle such a situation. The important point is to understand that your intent must be clear and rational, to avoid ambiguity in both the will's provisions and your mental state.

No matter how well you have planned, it is possible there will be debts owed when you die that will exceed the value of some of your bequests. Your debts must be paid before your bequests and the remaining residuary of your estate can be distributed to your beneficiaries named in the will. Unless you have directed in your will for such debts to be handled in a specific way, state law steps in to direct how the bills will be paid. This is called abatement of legacy.

Abatement by law occurs in a specific order. Generally, the residuary portion of the estate is utilized first to satisfy debts. If it is insufficient, general bequests are next, followed by specific bequests. The last portion to be attached is the spousal share. Except for the spousal share, you can leave instructions for a preferred order of abatement. This is an important point to discuss with your lawyer when you prepare your will. You can name entities and charities in your will, of course. When it comes to pets, be careful how you handle this in New York. If you make your pet Fluffy a direct beneficiary, Fluffy is not a "person." One way is to name a person in your will as a beneficiary who gets ownership and possession of Fluffy, along with a sum of money for Fluffy's care. For obvious reasons, this needs to be someone you trust to care for Fluffy — someone with whom you have discussed this plan when you made your will. Also, you should have a contingency in the will for if you outlive Fluffy.

A better approach is to create a pet trust to benefit Fluffy. Pet trusts are authorized by New York Code EPT section 7-8.1, which states in simple terms how the trust can be set up and administered. The statute provides the following:

(a) A trust for the care of a designated domestic or pet animal is valid. The intended use of the principal or income may be enforced by an individual designated for that purpose in the trust instrument or, if none, by an individual appointed by a court upon application to it by an individual, or by a trustee. Such trust shall terminate when the living animal beneficiary or beneficiaries of such trust are no longer alive.

(b) Except as expressly provided otherwise in the trust instrument, no portion of the principal or income may be converted to the use of the trustee or to any use other than for the benefit of all covered animals.

(c) Upon termination, the trustee shall transfer the unexpended trust property as directed in the trust instrument or, if there are no such directions in the trust instrument, the property shall pass to the estate of the grantor.

(d) A court may reduce the amount of the property transferred if it determines that amount substantially exceeds the amount required for the intended use. The amount of the reduction, if any, passes as unexpended trust property pursuant to paragraph (c) of this section.

(e) If no trustee is designated or no designated trustee is willing or able to serve, a court shall appoint a trustee and may make such other orders and determinations as are advisable to carry out the intent of the transferor and the purpose of this section."

You can set up a trust to take care of a pet or pets at the time of your death, which the court may examine to be reasonable or excessive, to cover the animal's care and disposal at the time of its death. In determining the amount for the trust, such factors as the animal's expected lifespan and support needs — such as veterinary costs, grooming, medicine, food, and board — must be factored into the estimate. If an extraordinary amount is set up for Fluffy way beyond Fluffy's needs, the New York court has the right to reduce the amount and direct the overage to your heirs. The key is to work with an experienced trust attorney to ensure you have covered your bases.

Bequests to Minors

Money and property of any significant value left to children under age 18 will be controlled by New York's Uniform Transfers to Minors Act (UTMA) unless you name a trustee of property for the minor. New York also recognizes your right to designate a personal guardian for minor children. Married parents frequently do this through creating mutual wills or appointing stand-by guardians.

Revocation of a Will

You may revoke your New York will by tearing it up, obliterating it, or otherwise destroying it with the intent to nullify it. You may revoke it by writing a new will. In the latter case, it is advisable to make the statement "all prior wills are revoked" just to make it easy to understand your intent.

People can inadvertently create will disputes by not clearly dating multiple wills and raising questions over which will prevails.

Divorce, dissolution, or annulment in New York automatically revokes a provision in a will that provides for that former spouse.

Intestate in New York

Probate law does not permit a vacuum. If a person dies without a valid will, New York law provides how the person's possessions — his estate — will be divided. As mentioned, in simple terms, if there is a surviving spouse, all will go to the surviving spouse — unless there are surviving children of the decedent who are not also the children of the surviving spouse. If there is at least one surviving child and surviving spouse, and the child is not the child of the surviving spouse, then the statute provides for a proportional division, which will change according to how many surviving children of the decedent are not related to the spouse. If there is no surviving spouse, but a surviving child — or parents, siblings, or other family members — then, depending on the relationship of the survivors to the decedent and in what numbers, the estate will be divided among them as prescribed by statute. The court will not take into consideration anything else, such as charities, nonrelatives, friends, or other relations that might have been important to the decedent, because New York law does not recognize such considerations or relationships — only next of kin.

Death Taxes

When making out your will and planning your estate, be sure to consult with your attorney and tax planner about the tax impact on your estate. This also will vary from state to state. New York follows the federal tax. Therefore, for 2010, the tax threshold is one million dollars. Federal legislation is pending for estate tax changes in 2011 and thereafter. New York might — or might not — continue to follow the federal tax scheme when the new law is enacted. Inheritance taxes might change as well, depending on where the estate tax lands. Stay close to your tax advisor on these issues if your estate is in the million-dollar ballpark.

How Your Will Might be Challenged

By now, you have an idea of the ways someone may challenge your will if you have not closed the loopholes when you prepared it. The ways such challenges most often arise are:

1. The document filed with the court is not a valid will because one or more of the following is missing: proper date, signature, or words indicating it is meant to be your last will and testament, or it is not properly witnessed by at least two competent witnesses who are not beneficiaries under the will.

2. You were not of sound mind when you wrote it.

3. Some part or all of the will does not comply with New York law.

4. Someone appears who claims to be your biological offspring — or a spouse — but who is not mentioned in the will.

5. Someone appears who claims to be your lawful spouse but who is not mentioned or is disinherited in the will.

6. Someone comes forward with a purported new will or codicil of a newer date.

7. The will is claimed to be a forgery or fraud.

If the will first presented to the probate court meets all the basic legal requirements — original document, dated, intent or agreement to be a will demonstrated, disposal of property contained within, signature, and proper witnesses to the signature — the court will presume the will to be valid unless and until proved otherwise. The challenger can file another will or codicil for the court to consider and evaluate, or can challenge the will itself, but the challenger must present evidence.

Perhaps the easiest challenge to a will is producing a more recent one that exhibits all the legal requirements, but where two wills are brought into question, it will often rest on the testimony of witnesses, and sometimes a handwriting expert for signatures, to determine which is the true will. The one of most recent date will be the controlling will if all other requirements of formation and execution are satisfied.

When you make a new will, you revoke all prior wills. When you make a codicil to an existing will, you only revoke a provision of the will that you are changing, not the entire will, because you are not making an entire new will when you prepare a codicil.

You can look ahead to potential challenges and prepare your will to prevent those challenges from having any effect on your wishes by preparing your will with the assistance of counsel to ensure it expresses your intent and meets the statutory requirements of a will.

A Different Type of Will — Your Living Will in New York

A "living will" is not about dispersing your property and stating your final wishes at the time of your death. It is about having your own control over your body if an accident or illness puts you in a medical situation in which it is difficult or impossible for you to speak for yourself in the moment. With a living will, a person can put in writing that he or she does not wish to be placed on life support systems if terminally ill or permanently unconscious (coma). The living will concept does not have the teeth of enforcement in all states. New York recognizes living wills and health care proxy forms.

A living will states that if you become permanently unable to participate in decisions regarding your medical care, the instructions you set forth in the living will document are to be followed by your family and health care providers. The key factors are that you:

1. Have a terminal condition,

2. Are permanently unconscious, or

3. Are conscious but have irreversible brain damage such that you cannot participate in the decision-making process of your medical care and life-saving measures.

You state in your living will that one of the above conditions applies and direct your instructions about the care you want, such as being made comfortable without extraordinary life support, no antibiotics, no cardiac resuscitation, no tube feeding, and/or no artificial respirator. There may be some measures you want taken and others you do not. Your living will is the document in which you prescribe and instruct your wishes in a clear and forthright manner. You also will appoint in your living will the person you want to be responsible to carry out your instructions as stated in the living will, and, ideally, a backup person as well. With the current privacy laws in place about personal health information, it is important to include this appointment in your living will document,

Make sure your appointed representative, physicians, caregivers, lawyer, and family have copies of your living will.

Similar in concept to a living will, but more encompassing in a broader context of situations (including organ and tissue donation), is the New York Health Care Proxy Form. In this document, you appoint an agent to act in your stead about health care decisions for you subject only to those limitations you put in the document. It is a revocable document. This person, as your "proxy," speaks for you in all health care matters.

Forms for both the New York Living Will and New York Health Care Proxy are available without cost on the New York Bar Association's Web site, at **www.nysba.org/Content/NavigationMenu/PublicResources/ LivingWillHealthCareProxyForms/Living_Will_and_Heal.htm.**

CHAPTER 12

Keeping it Current

Y ou have a will. All your trust documents are properly executed. Your brother has agreed to be your trustee, and your sister is his backup. Your cousin is your executor, with your aunt as backup. All guardians are on board. All your beneficiaries are alive and accounted for. Insurance policies are up-to-date. You have a living will and organ donation form in the hands of your doctor. All powers-of-attorney are ready, and your retirement is fully funded. But, unfortunately, putting together a comprehensive estate plan is just the first step. The good news is that the final step is less time-consuming.

The final step is to review your plan once a year or whenever there is a significant change that will affect your plan or beneficiaries. If you schedule a review when you change the batteries in your smoke detectors on the first day of spring or at the end of summer, you will have time to implement any updates that will take advantage of any changes in tax laws before the end of the fiscal year. The regular discipline means you will be able to take care of little changes quickly instead of having to go through the arduous process of making many changes all at one time.

After the volume of work that went into this plan, it might seem that a once-a-year review is quick and easy, but for those who wish to wash their hands of the whole business, that might seem too frequent. Your perspective is relative, so following the advice of those who know is a good idea. Most estate-planning professionals will tell you it is not a good idea to make many small changes throughout the year; it could get seriously expensive and complicated. A decision made in the midst of a difficult experience — such as eliminating a beneficiary from your estate — could result in a domino effect, with additional changes necessary, which will cost more time and stamina than you might have available. Change your mind again later, and the process starts all over.

The annual review sets a specific time for addressing issues that come up throughout the year. It also keeps your estate plan in the back of your mind. Just as you need to remember to change the oil in your car or the engine will blow up, you need to make changes to your estate plan, or it will not work the way you want it to. Once your estate plan is in place, maintenance can be simple.

What Changes?

It is not difficult to imagine the implication of some common life changes. Marriage, divorce, death of a beneficiary, the birth of a child, or losing your job will mean obvious changes to an estate plan: changing beneficiaries, including/removing a spouse on ownership documents, and updating your name if you legally change it. Other changes are going to require some thought and planning in order to make the necessary adjustments to your original plan.

Property:

- You give away or sell property specified in a will or trust.

- A natural disaster destroys or causes serious damage to a piece of real estate.

- You acquire a substantial amount of new property.

- Your home is robbed and property in your will is stolen.

Health:

- You or someone in your family is diagnosed with a life-threatening illness.

- You are hurt on the job.

- A parent becomes seriously ill and cannot afford medical care.

- The doctor gives you a clean bill of health, and you can go back to work.

Good news (with strings attached):

- Your daughter is accepted to Harvard but does not qualify for student loans.

- The adoption agency in Europe approved your five-year-old application, and you need to go pick up your son next week.

- Your trustee was transferred to Nepal with no set return date.

- Your wife received a promotion and you are moving to the West Coast, which is closer to her family.

Some of these situations could mean you need to take out a loan against your retirement savings, but others will involve the thoughtful work of choosing a new personal representative and getting the related documents up-to-date. Immediate needs ought to be addressed as they arise, such as naming a new trustee before heading to Europe to adopt your son, but some things can wait. Figuring out how to pay for a Harvard education and the implications it will have for your estate will take some time.

Check with the members of your estate-planning team to find out what kinds of changes they think ought to be addressed as quickly as possible and what can wait. Establish how you will communicate these things — e-mail notes to an assistant or a signed, original letter. Few finance-related companies will accept or execute directions left in a voicemail message, but maybe a message telling your advisor that an e-mail is coming and asking her to call when it arrives will suffice.

Once you are clear about the information you need to collect, make sure that you are keeping track of those pieces of information throughout the year. Consolidate and organize the information that will make it easy for you and your estate-planning team to have what they need. Create a file folder, make a running list, or designate a desk in your drawer for estate-planning essentials.

Make a copy of the acceptance letter from Harvard, staple to the back a print-out of the tuition and fee schedule you pulled from the Web site, and scribble notes to yourself for reference later: "Transfer stock from living trust? Sell time share?" If you are going to hand over documents to your lawyer or CPA, be sure to keep a copy for your files; if his gets lost or you need to discuss something over the phone, having a backup copy will make things simpler.

What Does "Maintenance" Look Like?

Your estate-planning team might be a group of two or 16 individuals in one or eight different companies. Regardless of their number, they are all likely to have an idea about how to coordinate your annual review, make changes, and handle documents. With that many people involved, the potential for disaster is only slightly limited by the fact that they all have a stake in making sure your plan remains intact and up to date. As the person with the estate, you need to decide what is most comfortable and reasonable for you.

A simple approach makes the most sense for something new — it will get complicated all by itself, so there is no need to help that along.

Make a list of each person in your estate-planning team along with their contact information, including company name and secondary contact. Then add the elements of your estate plan for which they are responsible.

The following is an example of how this contact sheet may look.

Pat Johnson, attorney at law
(Primary contact)
Dewey, Cheatum, and Howe
1234 Jokester Lane, Suite 6789
New York, New York 55555
513-555-1234 – Office
513-558-1098 – Direct line
513-555-2345 – Fax
513-555-3456 – Mobile
513-555-4567 – Home/emergency

Gail Silver, attorney at law
(Secondary contact)
Dewey, Cheatum, and Howe
1234 Jokester Lane, Suite 6789
New York, New York 55555
513-555-1234 – Office
513-555-9876 – Direct line
513-555-2345 – Fax
513-555-8765 – Mobile
513-555-7654 – Home/emergency

** If neither contact is available, call the main number and explain the situation. The receptionist will find an alternative contact for immediate assistance. **

Hours: M-F 8 a.m.-6 p.m., Sat. – by appointment, Sun. – closed
Documents: Will, living will, and organ donation documents
Stored: Dewey's document vault

Once your list is compiled, look over all the contacts and decide who would make the best point person or coordinator among the group. This person will serve as the top of the phone tree; in the case of a need or emergency, you only have one person to call who will inform the rest, so you only have to say things once. It is similar to a snow day: One parent has a short list of people to call to say that school is closed, and each of those people has a short list. That way, everyone finds out rather quickly that it is a day for sledding. In the case of your estate plan, if one meeting is preferred, then your point person will collect and prepare all the documents needed from each person on the team so that you do not have to run all over town. The person who takes on this responsibility might charge a fee for this work, but when you are short on time, the convenience is well worth the investment.

Next, you need to choose a date for that annual review. If you only have two people with whom to meet, you could schedule back-to-back appointments on the same day and take care of your work for the year. The timing of this review will depend as much on your goals for your estate plan as it will on the space in your calendar. If taxes are a primary concern, then schedule your review at a point in the year that will allow you to have enough time to review the changes and make and implement decisions to maximize your savings or minimize your payments. If trusts are a big part of your estate, then the same kind of review will be needed to address any changes in trust regulations.

The likelihood of having time to do a review at the end of the year might be unrealistic — trying to squeeze in the appointments necessary between holiday parties, shopping, visits by out-of-town family, and inclement weather in some parts of the country can be a challenge. But then spring is a busy time, too, with breaks in school schedules and getting ready for graduations and summer vacations. There are more uses of your time than you thought imaginable when it comes to setting up a review of your estate plan. Ask your advisors what they think.

Periodic updates each quarter might help define when the annual review ought to happen. If a new tax law is passed in February, then an update from your CPA in March will give you plenty of time to reach and consider the implications before the annual review you schedule for early September — the kids are back in school, and the holiday rush has not yet begun. This kind of attention to your plan throughout the year will make the annual sit-down less involved.

If you have your planners get in touch with you a month or two in advance of your meeting, in addition to reminding you that it is coming, this will allow you to give them some directions about documents that need to be prepared. Following are a few examples of what could be happening that would be important to pass along:

- Your daughter Elizabeth just had a baby — Jeremy Jason Wolf — so you want to create a trust just like the one you have for all the other grandchildren. He also needs to be added to your will.

- Grandma Sophie passed away unexpectedly the week after Jeremy arrived; something needs to be done about her trust for assisted-living expenses, and you need to consider suggestions about what to do with it. She also needs to be taken out of your will, with Grandpa George as the new beneficiary for her bequests.

- Kelley dropped out of business school to pursue an arts training program — will her education trust be able to cover her expenses, even though the apprenticeship-like institution is not accredited?

You could sit down and sign the necessary documents at your review. Some of your team members might regard the review as the time to go over all that information and follow up with the document signing later. Keeping your team in the loop about what is happening in your life is important so that they can manage your estate plan, but you need to make sure that communication, again, supports your estate-plan goals. An e-mail or phone call when something significant occurs might be essential. Then again, waiting might not make much difference to your plan; it could save you considerable hassle given the number of times you would have to make those contacts.

What to Go Over

You need to go over all elements of your estate plan. Until the documents and routine become familiar, it could be easy to forget some of them. *The estate planning worksheets in Appendix A assist in identifying the components of your estate plan.* These components might include:

Last will and testament

Living will

Health care proxy

Organ donor form/card

Guardians for children

Guardians for others

Life insurance policies

Disability insurance policies

Other insurance policies

Trust: For spouse

Trust: For children

Trust: For retirement

Trust: For pet(s)

Trust: For charity _____

Trust: For charity _____

Trust: Living _____

Trust: Pourover to probate estate

Real property — joint tenancy with survivorship

Real property — subject to homestead exemption

Real property — out of state

Real property — _____
POD accounts/stocks/etc.
Retirement: 401(k)/pension/Keogh
Stock portfolio/investments

You will also want to consider your executor and backup, trustees and their backups, and anything else that is people-related. The goal is to make sure your documents reflect your wishes so that after you are gone, no matter when that happens, your estate is disposed of the way you want. It also helps the people you leave behind, so you need to address with your estate-planning team how to make sure those things happen.

Your Desk

Federal law requires individuals and businesses to retain documentation that supports tax returns for a specific number of years. Anyone who has had to go through an audit learns the hard way that this is not merely a guideline. Estate-planning documents could be considered more important than your tax records because they are the legal record dictating the disposal of your property, and what happens to that directly affects the taxes paid by your estate and every one of your beneficiaries. Stuffing those things into a cubby of an over-stuffed roll-top desk, and forgetting about them is not wise. Imagine your family trying to find the name of your lawyer in such a mess.

How to organize your documents and information is a personal matter. One file folder of everything might suffice, whereas a separate folder for each estate-planning team member might work best. Or, you might assign one folder per document or plan element so that the history of all changes is readily accessible. Whatever method you choose, be sure to include any information your family might need to access after your death. You should include the following information:

- **Contact information**: Company name, phone number, fax, e-mail address, and any other information that you use to manage these accounts

- **Payment information**: Account numbers, usual due dates, and method of payment for any bills — automatic deductions from your checking or savings; online bill payment via your bank, coupon book, and checks mailed

- **Debts/accounts**:

  — **Real estate**: Home mortgage, second mortgage, timeshare, vacation property, and investment property
  — **Loans**: Line of credit, signature loans, and credit cards
  — Utilities: Gas, electric, water, sewer, heating oil, telephone, cell phone, Internet service provider, and cable/satellite
  — **Regular payments**: Car payment, insurance, automatic deposits into savings or other accounts, magazine subscriptions, and newspaper delivery

- **Resources**:

  — **Income**: Payroll checks, rental income, structured settlement, royalties, annuity payments, and retirement distributions
  — **Bank accounts**: Checking, savings, and certificates of deposit (CDs)
  — **Investments**: Money market accounts

The inventory worksheet in Appendix A will help you begin assembling this information. If you already keep individual file folders for these documents so that you have a place to put the stubs from the electric company or receipts from the company that delivers your heating oil, then indicate the name and location of the folder. Also note if there is a monthly payment book or the electronic delivery of notices instead of traditional mail delivery.

The truly meticulous will want to have a centralized place for the original paperwork created when an account was set up, correspondences, and any other historical documents. When an executor of an estate is contacted about an outstanding debt, having access to that kind of information could make his or her job much easier.

Unfortunately, this kind of consolidation also makes it easier for a thief or unscrupulous family member to gain access to your assets. For this reason, it is important to keep these documents in a secure location. A fire-resistant home safe or locking file cabinet will make the materials readily available to you, but a greater challenge for someone else to access.

• *Did You Know?* •

If you want to be buried instead of cremated after you are gone, you need to let your wishes be known. A former queen of England prepared every detail of her funeral, including the conveyance of her coffin to the church and who would be invited to have a seat in a pew.

Another royal, not held in high esteem at the palace, died unexpectedly, so a funeral had to be prepared fast. The good news is that just such a funeral plan was ready; the bad news was mostly for the former queen who planned it — all her work was going to be used by someone else.

Most people will not need a protocol book for their final arrangements, but having things done your way will require you to make your wishes known. Planning your own funeral could seem a bit morbid, but look at it this way: You plan your birthday party, so why not plan your last party, too?

One Last Motivator: Probate and You

One big reason to make sure your estate plan is up-to-date is for avoiding or minimizing probate court proceedings, even though the process is no longer the nightmare it used to be. Probate procedure is designed to settle your debts and distribute your assets with certainty.

After your death, your executor is required to file your will with the probate court in the appropriate jurisdictions. The following are general laws relating to probate:

- If a person dies without a will, an administrator — or executor — is appointed by the judge. If the person dies with a will but does not use will alternatives, such as trusts, to distribute assets to beneficiaries, then the all estate assets will fall to the named executor to guide through the court process.

- The court posts a notice of your death, most often in local and regional papers and in the courthouse to notify creditors of your death and allows a set time period for claims to be made against the estate. Once the defined window of time is closed, no more requests for payment will be considered.

- The executor/administrator notifies all beneficiaries and creditors of the estate that the administration of the will is going forward.

- The executor/administrator collects all the assets and prepares a list or inventory. Court approval must be sought to sell any assets in order to pay debts or make bequests.

- The executor/administrator reviews and pays all outstanding debts.

- The executor/administrator pays all taxes.

- The executor/administrator distributes the remaining assets according to the order of the court.

If the individual dies intestate, the court will designate heirs. If there is a will and the probate process is used to settle the estate, then the court can also make orders about which of the beneficiaries receives what. If a particular asset that was identified as a bequest has to be sold to pay taxes, then the court might order that the beneficiary of that asset be given something else, or that the person gets nothing.

Circumstances that influence the probate process do arise, and how each court in various states will handle these might be different. In the case of murder, most states — including New York — will not permit someone who intentionally kills a person to inherit any portion of the deceased person's estate; this includes receiving the proceeds from a life insurance policy, trust, or other arrangement.

In the case of adultery or abandonment, some intestate laws will not allow the spouse who cheated or deserted to inherit anything from the estate. The evidence needed to make the case for either situation varies. One distinction is clear in most states: A missing spouse is different from abandonment. A spouse who has not voluntarily moved out but is gone without any explanation can be declared missing. A period of years must pass — the minimum amount of time varies by state — before any legal action can be taken. The family can then request that a person be declared legally dead, making it possible to execute a will, receive insurance benefits, and proceed with other estate-related activities.

The advantage of probate court is that if you have a feuding family or just do not care what happens to your belongings when you are gone, the state will take care of it for you. If either case is true, then you can save yourself the work of the annual review process. If you prefer to direct things yourself, the annual review process can prevent extensive probate involvement.

If you name a beneficiary for a trust or insurance policy, and that person declines the bequest or is dead, the secondary beneficiary will inherit. If you do not have a secondary beneficiary named, then the probate court will settle the matter. Any issues that you do not account for in your will, will alternatives, or other estate-distribution activities will be settled by the probate court.

Taking a few hours each year to make sure your documents are in place and up-to-date is a small investment compared to the effort those who are left behind must expend.

Identity Theft

As you collect information about all your assets and liabilities and compile important personal information, it is important to be aware of safeguarding the related documentation. Identify theft is a quite real, dangerous threat. A person representing himself or herself as another individual is a crime that can be prevented. When you do not think like a criminal, it can be difficult to figure out what you need to do to protect yourself.

Some of the ways in which a skilled identity thief will steal your information might surprise you. The following are ways to consider:

- **Change of address**: By submitting a change-of-address card with the U.S. Postal Service (USPS), the thief will send your mail to a location where he or she can get at it without suspicion.

- **Stealing**: Taking mail out of your mailbox is a bit more risky, but it does happen. Completing and returning pre-approved credit cards with a change of address is just one way your mail can be used to steal your identity (along with stealing your wallet, taking personal records from an employer, or offering bribes to employees who have access to sell your information).

- **Garbage diving**: This is the act of looking through trash to find bills or bank statements with account information or any personal information that might be useful in the act of stealing someone's identity, such as a social security number, mother's maiden name, or personal identification number (PIN). This is not considered theft; the U.S. Supreme Court has ruled that anything left out for trash collection is in the public domain.

- **Skimming**: This is accomplished by using a special high-tech storage device that electronically "grabs" your account number and other personal information when a store computer is processing your credit card purchase/transaction.

Avoiding identity theft

If you want to avoid being robbed on the street, there are some common-sense things you can do without going to a "How Not to Get Mugged" class. Do not walk alone in a strange neighborhood at night, and only park in brightly lit parking lots. Like these behaviors, there are some obvious things people do that help prevent identify theft, such as cutting up old credit cards instead of throwing them into the trash intact. However, if you throw all the pieces into the same garbage bag, a thief can reassemble the pieces and make Internet purchases because he will have access to the security code on the back of the card.

Through the unfortunate experiences of those who have had their credit rating destroyed, among other unfortunate consequences, the methods of identity thieves are no longer a secret. There are many things you can do to avoid being robbed of your good name.

The first and most important thing is awareness: Pay attention to what you are doing with your personal information. If you are scribbling notes about the accounts you need to look up and then jot them down on a piece of paper so that you can enter them into a spreadsheet, do not throw that paper into the trash. Create a pile or special trash can for "personal info." Put anything that needs to be disposed of in that one place, such as old utility bills, bank statements from an account you closed ten years ago, or statements from your insurance company telling you that a reimbursement has been made to your primary-care physician. Then choose a method for making those documents unreadable.

Invest in a small, crosscut shredder — because larger scraps of paper can be reassembled like a puzzle. Remember the news clips of federal investigators hauling out bags of shredded documents from a national corporation under investigation? If your documents are not old and dusty, call your local animal shelter and ask whether they can use shredded paper for litter boxes. It is not very likely a thief is going to want to go through that much effort to go through your documents once the cats, dogs, or guinea pigs are done with them. Most shredders will also destroy credit cards — make sure you do not mix your plastic with paper going to the shelter. If you want to be super-safe with your credit card bits, separate the plastic bits into several different trash cans and dispose of them at different times.

Burning paper until it is a powdery ash also works well. Some other ways to prevent identity theft are equally simple, once you have them in mind.

- Never give out personal information to a stranger over the telephone or via blind mailers. If you want to register an appliance or request more information from a company, call them. Do not fill out a postcard that asks for your e-mail address, birthdate, or other personal data that can be read and copied by anyone who sees it.

- Treat your social security number like gold; guard it the same way you would a gold coin. Do not carry your social security card in your wallet or purse, and never write it on a check. Only provide it when absolutely necessary, and then only to someone you have verified as an authorized agent for the company with whom you share it.

- Passwords for any account need to be unusual — do not use the birthdates of your children, your wedding anniversary, any portion of your social security number, or your telephone number. Some of that information is easy to obtain through public records requests, and it will provide open access to your accounts.

- Never communicate personal information via e-mail. If you need to get the information to someone quickly, call and leave a message in a private voicemail box or send a fax to a confidential location where the information will not be handled by many people. If e-mail is a necessary means for communicating, never send complete information in one e-mail: send most of your social security number in one e-mail, and send the last four digits in a second e-mail. Same with account numbers — even better is to e-mail part and call with the remainder. Electronic communications should not be considered secure — they can be intercepted or read by someone other than your intended audience.

- If a delivery person says she is with the U.S. Postal Service (USPS) but is stopping by to drop off a package for her friend on her way home after changing out of her uniform, refuse the package and tell her your usual letter carrier can come back tomorrow in uniform, and you will sign for it then. If that feels like being paranoid and untrusting, that is all right. You would not give your child to a stranger, so do not give yourself either, in the form of your personal information.

Be on the lookout

First and foremost, this means to protect any official documents or written materials — such as the completed worksheets from this book — so that nobody has access to them unless you grant them permission. A locking file cabinet with a limited number of keys that are not numbered is one option. Standard file cabinets, like the ones you can get from a large manufacturer, have a number written on the lock. If you lose the key, you can give them that number and a few dollars and they will send a replacement — but they will do the same for a thief, no questions asked.

A fire-resistant safe or lockbox that you can store at home will also work. Those safes are not fireproof, meaning whatever is inside will not necessarily survive in any fire. Fire-resistant means what is inside will be protected for a number of hours before the safe itself gets so hot that flammable material will catch fire and disintegrate. Portable boxes can also be stolen. None of this means you should not bother with these options; it just means you should be aware of the limitations of your choices.

Other choices you have for protection are being on the lookout for unusual problems:

- You are denied credit when you think your credit rating is sound.

- Bills or other information, such as letters or warranty offers, arrive for purchases you did not make.

- Bills that come at the same time every month or related to a specific purchase do not arrive as anticipated.

- Credit cards or account statements for which you did not apply are delivered.

If any of these events happen, investigate. Along those same lines, request a copy of your credit report on a regular basis, at least once a year, and check it for unusual activity; immediately follow up on anything that is suspicious. Federal law now requires nationwide credit reporting agencies to provide one free copy of your credit report each year, upon request. Visit **www.annualcreditreport.com** or call 1-877-322-8228 and request your free report. You can also write to:

Annual Credit Report Request Service
PO Box 105281
Atlanta, GA 30348-5281

Review any statements you get about existing accounts — credit card, checking, savings, money market — and see whether there is anything out of place. If something is wrong, or some vital information is stolen, act immediately.

Close any accounts that have been set up in your name but not by your doing or any account of yours that has been meddled with. Report the trouble immediately to your local police by filing a police report. Prepare an ID Theft Affidavit with the Federal Trade Commission, available via **www.ftc.gov/IDtheft**, or report it via telephone at 1-877-ID-THEFT (438-4338) or TTY 1-866-653-4261. Traditional mail is also an option:

Identity Theft Clearinghouse
Federal Trade Commission
Washington. D.C. 20580

You can also place a "Fraud Alert" on your credit report; this instructs creditors to follow specific procedures before a new account is opened in your name. They will also follow these procedures when a change of personal information is requested. Before any action is taken, you can receive a phone call that will require the verification of a combination of specific personal information that would be difficult for a thief to have all at one time. There are only a few national credit reporting companies, so calling one company will let the others know that an alert has been requested — no need for you to call all three.

Equifax: 1-800-525-6285
Experian: 1-800-397-3742
TransUnion: 1-800-680-7289

Identity theft is a threat that ought to be taken seriously. Educate yourself and your family, and you will reduce your chances of being victimized.

Additional resources:

- About identity theft:

  - Federal Trade Commission: **www.ftc.gov/idtheft**
  - Identity Theft Resource Center: **www.idtheftcenter.org**
  - Social Security Administration: **www.socialsecurity.gov/pubs/10064.pdf**

- For victims of identity theft:

  - Privacy Rights Clearinghouse: **www.privacyrights.org**
  - Office of Justice Programs, Office for Victims of Crimes (OVC): **www.ojp.usdoj.gov/ovc/help/it.htm**

CONCLUSION

Congratulations: You have an estate to plan. It turns out that you do not have to be rich, famous, or pompous to have the kind of resources that make it necessary to plan for the future.

The single most important thing you can do now is to create an estate plan. Even if you have done all the exercises in this book, you know there is much more work to do. The work that is necessary to move from where you are now to the point where you are scheduling regular annual meetings with estate professionals might seem a monumental task. However, the good news is that it can be done. You have enough information to ask informed questions and begin to narrow down this huge idea of estate planning into your goals, will, and trusts.

The need to create your own definitions is why you did not find sample wills, a standard trust document, or an annuity template in these pages; it is counterproductive. Trying to shoe-horn your information into a prescribed form supports a cookie-cutter approach to something that is highly personal — you are the one who loses with that kind of approach. The things you want to accomplish with the results of your years of hard work are not going to be like those of your brother Ben or your sister Sally. There will always be similarities, which is why books like this exist, but they need to serve as a place to begin, not end.

Customization takes time and might stir up considerable emotion — maybe even issues you would rather not face. Take your time and get the help you need with all of it. If you set your own pace and find people with whom you are comfortable, you will avoid unnecessary frustration, upset, and expense.

So, build in some fun to get yourself through the difficult things. Every time you reach a milestone, like completing your will, treat yourself to a dinner out or spend a day lounging under a tree, reading a book, or enjoying your favorite type of outing. Always remind yourself of the gifts you give that cannot be delineated in writing — your wish to make your departure less burdensome, your thoughtfulness, and your love for the people in your life are all communicated through the effort of this work.

APPENDIX A

Estate-Planning Worksheets

Your Estate in Black and White

Page 1

Name _____ Birth _____ SS# _____

Spouse _____ Birth _____ SS# _____

Primary Address _____ # of Minors _____

Child _____ Birth _____ SS# _____

Child _____ Birth _____ SS# _____

Guardian of _____ Birth _____ SS# _____

ASSETS				
Real Estate: *primary residence, vacation home, land*				
Address/ Description	Ownership	Mortgage(s)	Purchase Price/Year	**Current Value**

Automobile(s)				
Year	Make	Model	Ownership	**Current Value**

Accounts: *checking, savings, certificate of deposit, brokerage*			
Type	Beneficiary(ies)	Account #	**Current Value**

Life Insurance					
Company	Insured	Beneficiary(ies)	Ownership	Face Value	**Current Value**

Retirement: *401(k), IRA, Roth IRA, Keogh, pension, profit sharing, social security*				
Plan	Ownership	Beneficiary(ies)	**Vested Year/ Percent**	**Current Value**

Other Financial Assets: *stocks, bond, inheritance, structured settlement, rent payments*			
Type	Beneficiary(ies)	Ownership	**Current Value**

Personal Property: *boat/jet ski, jewelry, artwork, antiques, collectibles, household contents, etc.*			
Type	Value	Purchase Year	**Current Value**

Page 2

ADDITIONAL ASSETS			
List all of the things that did not fit on previous page of the inventory sheet:			
Type	Value	Purchase Year	Current Value

$ _____

Total Assets $ _____

LIABILITIES			
First mortgage, second mortgage, line of credit, car loan, and credit card balance, for example:			
Type	Ownership	Due/Payoff Year	Current Value

Total Liabilities $ _____

Total Assets $ _____

Total Liabilities — $ _____

Total Net Worth = $ _____

Prioritization

This is about making choices regarding what you can and cannot do with your estate. Indicate your six key values. These are the values or qualities to which you are attracted:

1.	
2.	
3.	
4.	
5.	
6.	

Then, add the one key value to orient your life around: _____

_____

Now list all of the things you would like to accomplish with your estate planning, and connect those with your highest values: If more than one value is accomplished, note that.

		Goals	Value
1.	$5k	*Leave a substantial amount of money to cat shelter*	*Involvement*
2.	$50k	*Education funds for niece and nephews*	*Education*
3.	$		
4.	$		
5.	$		
6.	$		
7.	$		
8.	$		
9.	$		
10.	$		
11.	$		

After you have completed your list of goals, place an approximate dollar value for the gift you would like to leave in the left-hand margin. Use a range if you are not sure.

Total Gifts $ _____

Match this up against your list of assets and see how close the dollar amounts are. If the numbers are nowhere near each other, then you might need to consider investing to build up your estate or changing the priorities in your list.

If they are close, consider what decisions need to be made to make a cash contribution, the transfer of real estate, or the value of property. If you list $500,000 in cash, are you willing or able to sell your house to come up with the money? Could you donate your house to a charitable institution in place of a cash donation? Would your family contest your will and challenge your wishes if the house has been in the family for generations? These are the details you need to discuss with your estate planner.

Who, What, How, and When

After you decide on the people and organizations to receive a bequest, take a moment to write out your list. This will be useful when you sit down with your estate planning team to finalize the paperwork and implementation of your estate plan. Leave any places blank if you are unsure.

Who/ relationship	What Circumstances	How	When	Special
Jeanine/niece	*$50,000 + books ($10k value)*	*Trust (bequest)*	*2010*	*Will*
Cat shelter/charity	*$5,000*	*Bequest*	*2010*	*Will*
Danny/brother	*$250,000*	*Living trust/bequest*	*2010*	*Will*

Essential Documents and Accounts Inventory

Life will go on after you die, and handling your estate will likely fall to people who are mired in grief. To make it easier to find and deal with the accounts and obligations you leave behind, consolidate as much information as possible. This worksheet is a place to begin compiling that data.

This information will also be helpful to have when you meet with your estate planner.

DEBTS
Mortgage
Company Name:
Account Number:
Contact:
Phone Number:
E-mail Address:

Payment Amount:
Usual Due Date:
Method of Payment: *(automatic deductions for checking/savings, online bill payment via bank, coupon with check)*
PIN: *(Personal identification number)*
Secret Question:
Answer:
Second Mortgage
Company Name:
Account Number:
Contact:
Phone Number:
E-mail Address:
Payment Amount:
Usual Due Date:
Method of Payment:
PIN:
Secret Question:
Answer:
Timeshare — Mortgage Information
Company Name:
Account Number:
Contact:
Phone Number:
E-mail Address:
Payment Amount:
Usual Due Date:
Method of Payment:
PIN:
Secret Question:
Answer:
Vacation Property — Mortgage Information
Company Name:
Account Number:
Contact:
Phone Number:
E-mail Address:

Payment Amount:	
Usual Due Date:	
Method of Payment:	
PIN:	
Secret Question:	
Answer:	
Loans — Home Equity	
Company Name:	
Account Number:	
Contact:	
Phone Number:	
E-mail Address:	
Payment Amount:	
Usual Due Date:	
Method of Payment:	
PIN:	
Secret Question:	
Answer:	
Loans — Line of Credit	
Company Name:	
Account Number:	
Contact:	
Phone Number:	
E-mail Address:	
Payment Amount:	
Usual Due Date:	
Method of Payment:	
PIN:	
Secret Question:	
Answer:	
Loans — Signature	
Company Name:	
Account Number:	
Contact:	
Phone Number:	
E-mail Address:	
Payment Amount:	

Usual Due Date:	
Method of Payment:	
PIN:	
Secret Question:	
Answer:	
Loans — Student / College Tuition	
Company Name:	
Account Number:	
Contact:	
Phone Number:	
E-mail Address:	
Payment Amount:	
Usual Due Date:	
Method of Payment:	
PIN:	
Secret Question:	
Answer:	
Loans — Automobile	
Company Name:	
Account Number:	
Contact:	
Phone Number:	
E-mail Address:	
Payment Amount:	
Usual Due Date:	
Method of Payment:	
PIN:	
Secret Question:	
Answer:	
Loans — Other (boat, second car, etc.)	
Company Name:	
Account Number:	
Contact:	
Phone Number:	
E-mail Address:	
Payment Amount:	
Usual Due Date:	

Method of Payment:	
PIN:	
Secret Question:	
Answer:	
Credit Card #1	
Company Name:	
Account Number:	
Contact:	
Phone Number:	
E-mail Address:	
Payment Amount:	
Usual Due Date:	
Method of Payment:	
PIN:	
Secret Question:	
Answer:	
Credit Card #2	
Company Name:	
Account Number:	
Contact:	
Phone Number:	
E-mail Address:	
Payment Amount:	
Usual Due Date:	
Method of Payment:	
PIN:	
Secret Question:	
Answer:	
Credit Card #3	
Company Name:	
Account Number:	
Contact:	
Phone Number:	
E-mail Address:	
Payment Amount:	
Usual Due Date:	

Method of Payment:	
PIN:	
Secret Question:	
Answer:	
Other — Account 1	
Company Name:	
Account Number:	
Contact:	
Phone Number:	
E-mail Address:	
Payment Amount:	
Usual Due Date:	
Method of Payment:	
PIN:	
Secret Question:	
Answer:	
Other — Account 2	
Company Name:	
Account Number:	
Contact:	
Phone Number:	
E-mail Address:	
Payment Amount:	
Usual Due Date:	
Method of Payment:	
PIN:	
Secret Question:	
Answer:	
Other — Account 3	
Company Name:	
Account Number:	
Contact:	
Phone Number:	
E-mail Address:	
Payment Amount:	
Usual Due Date:	
Method of Payment:	

PIN:	
Secret Question:	
Answer:	

LIVING EXPENSES

Gas and Electric

Company Name:	
Account Number:	
Contact:	
Phone Number:	
E-mail Address:	
Payment Amount:	
Usual Due Date:	
Method of Payment:	
PIN:	
Secret Question:	
Answer:	

Water and Sewer or Septic

Company Name:	
Account Number:	
Contact:	
Phone Number:	
E-mail Address:	
Payment Amount:	
Usual Due Date:	
Method of Payment:	
PIN:	
Secret Question:	
Answer:	

Telephone

Company Name:	
Account Number:	
Contact:	
Phone Number:	
E-mail Address:	
Payment Amount:	
Usual Due Date:	

Method of Payment:	
PIN:	
Secret Question:	
Answer:	
Heating Oil	
Company Name:	
Account Number:	
Contact:	
Phone Number:	
E-mail Address:	
Payment Amount:	
Usual Due Date:	
Method of Payment:	
PIN:	
Secret Question:	
Answer:	
Internet Service Provider (ISP)	
Company Name:	
Account Number:	
Contact:	
Phone Number:	
E-mail Address:	
Payment Amount:	
Usual Due Date:	
Method of Payment:	
PIN:	
Secret Question:	
Answer:	
Cable / Satellite Television Service	
Company Name:	
Account Number:	
Contact:	
Phone Number:	
E-mail Address:	
Payment Amount:	
Usual Due Date:	

Method of Payment:
PIN:
Secret Question:
Answer:
Other — Account 1
Company Name:
Account Number:
Contact:
Phone Number:
E-mail Address:
Payment Amount:
Usual Due Date:
Method of Payment:
PIN:
Secret Question:
Answer:
Other — Account 2
Company Name:
Account Number:
Contact:
Phone Number:
E-mail Address:
Payment Amount:
Usual Due Date:
Method of Payment:
PIN:
Secret Question:
Answer:
OTHER REGULAR PAYMENTS
Insurance: Life — Policy 1
Company Name:
Account Number:
Contact:
Phone Number:
E-mail Address:
Payment Amount:
Usual Due Date:

Method of Payment:	
PIN:	
Secret Question:	
Answer:	
Insurance: Life — Policy 2	
Company Name:	
Account Number:	
Contact:	
Phone Number:	
E-mail Address:	
Payment Amount:	
Usual Due Date:	
Method of Payment:	
PIN:	
Secret Question:	
Answer:	
Insurance: Life — Disability (Long/Short-Term)	
Company Name:	
Account Number:	
Contact:	
Phone Number:	
E-mail Address:	
Payment Amount:	
Usual Due Date:	
Method of Payment:	
PIN:	
Secret Question:	
Answer:	
Insurance: Homeowner's / Renter's	
Company Name:	
Account Number:	
Contact:	
Phone Number:	
E-mail Address:	
Payment Amount:	
Usual Due Date:	

Method of Payment:	
PIN:	
Secret Question:	
Answer:	
Insurance: Car — Policy 1	
Company Name:	
Account Number:	
Contact:	
Phone Number:	
E-mail Address:	
Payment Amount:	
Usual Due Date:	
Method of Payment:	
PIN:	
Secret Question:	
Answer:	
Insurance: Car — Policy 2	
Company Name:	
Account Number:	
Contact:	
Phone Number:	
E-mail Address:	
Payment Amount:	
Usual Due Date:	
Method of Payment:	
PIN:	
Secret Question:	
Answer:	
Newspaper Subscription 1	
Company Name:	
Account Number:	
Contact:	
Phone Number:	
E-mail Address:	
Payment Amount:	
Usual Due Date:	
Method of Payment:	

Newspaper Subscription 2
Company Name:
Account Number:
Contact:
Phone Number:
E-mail Address:
Payment Amount:
Usual Due Date:
Method of Payment:
Magazine Subscription 1
Company Name:
Account Number:
Contact:
Phone Number:
E-mail Address:
Payment Amount:
Usual Due Date:
Method of Payment:
Magazine Subscription 2
Company Name:
Account Number:
Contact:
Phone Number:
E-mail Address:
Payment Amount:
Usual Due Date:
Method of Payment:
Magazine Subscription 3
Company Name:
Account Number:
Contact:
Phone Number:
E-mail Address:
Payment Amount:
Usual Due Date:
Method of Payment:
Other — Account 1

Company Name:	
Account Number:	
Contact:	
Phone Number:	
E-mail Address:	
Payment Amount:	
Usual Due Date:	
Method of Payment:	
PIN:	
Secret Question:	
Answer:	
Other — Account 2	
Company Name:	
Account Number:	
Contact:	
Phone Number:	
E-mail Address:	
Payment Amount:	
Usual Due Date:	
Method of Payment:	
PIN:	
Secret Question:	
Answer:	
INCOME	
Payroll Check 1	
Company Name:	
Account Number:	
Contact:	
Phone Number:	
E-mail Address:	
Check Amount:	
Pay Day/Dates:	
Method of Payment: *(check, direct deposit, cash, other)*	
Additional Important Information:	

Payroll Check 2
Company Name:
Account Number:
Contact:
Phone Number:
E-mail Address:
Check Amount:
Pay Day/Dates:
Method of Payment: *(check, direct deposit, cash, other)*
Additional Important Information:

Structured Settlement
Company Name:
Account Number:
Contact:
Phone Number:
E-mail Address:
Check Amount:
Day/Dates Paid:
Method of Payment: *(check, direct deposit, cash, other)*
Additional Important Information:

Royalty Payment 1
Company Name:
Account Number:
Contact:
Phone Number:
E-mail Address:
Check Amount:
Day/Dates Paid:
Method of Payment: *(check, direct deposit, cash, other)*
Additional Important Information:

Royalty Payment 2
Company Name:

Account Number:
Contact:
Phone Number:
E-mail Address:
Check Amount:
Day/Dates Paid:
Method of Payment: *(check, direct deposit, cash, other)*
Additional Important Information:

Annuity Payment 1
Company Name:
Account Number:
Contact:
Phone Number:
E-mail Address:
Check Amount:
Day/Dates Paid:
Method of Payment: *(check, direct deposit, cash, other)*
Additional Important Information:

Annuity Payment 2
Company Name:
Account Number:
Contact:
Phone Number:
E-mail Address:
Check Amount:
Day/Dates Paid:
Method of Payment: *(check, direct deposit, cash, other)*
Additional Important Information:

Retirement Distribution — Plan 1
Company Name:
Account Number:
Contact:

Phone Number:	
E-mail Address:	
Check Amount:	
Day/Dates Paid:	
Method of Payment: *(check, direct deposit, cash, other)*	
Additional Important Information:	
Retirement Distribution — Plan 2	
Company Name:	
Account Number:	
Contact:	
Phone Number:	
E-mail Address:	
Check Amount:	
Day/Dates Paid:	
Method of Payment: *(check, direct deposit, cash, other)*	
Rental Property 1	
Company Name:	
Account Number:	
Contact:	
Phone Number:	
E-mail Address:	
Check Amount:	
Day/Dates Paid:	
Method of Payment: *(check, direct deposit, cash, other)*	
Tenant Information:	
Rental Property 2	
Company Name:	
Account Number:	
Contact:	
Phone Number:	
E-mail Address:	
Check Amount:	

Day/Dates Paid:	
Method of Payment: *(check, direct deposit, cash, other)*	
Tenant Information:	

FINANCIAL RESOURCES

Checking — Account 1

Financial Institution:	
Account Number:	
Contact:	
Phone Number:	
E-mail Address:	
Balance:	
Date:	
PIN:	
Secret Question:	
Answer:	
Additional Important Information:	

Checking — Account 2

Financial Institution:	
Account Number:	
Contact:	
Phone Number:	
E-mail Address:	
Balance:	
Date:	
PIN:	
Secret Question:	
Answer:	
Additional Important Information:	

Savings — Account 1

Financial Institution:	
Account Number:	
Contact:	
Phone Number:	

E-mail Address:
Balance:
Date:
PIN:
Secret Question:
Answer:
Additional Important Information:

Savings — Account 2
Financial Institution;
Account Number:
Contact:
Phone Number:
E-mail Address:
Balance:
Date:
PIN:
Secret Question:
Answer:
Additional Important Information:

Certificate of Deposit — Account 1
Financial Institution:
Account Number:
Contact:
Phone Number:
E-mail Address:
Balance:
Date:
PIN:
Secret Question:
Answer:
Additional Important Information:

Certificate of Deposit — Account 2
Financial Institution:
Account Number:

Contact:	
Phone Number:	
E-mail Address:	
Balance:	
Date:	
PIN:	
Secret Question:	
Answer:	
Additional Important Information:	

Money Market Fund — Account 1

Financial Institution:	
Account Number:	
Contact:	
Phone Number:	
E-mail Address:	
Balance:	
Date:	
PIN:	
Secret Question:	
Answer:	
Additional Important Information:	

Money Market Fund — Account 2

Financial Institution:	
Account Number:	
Contact:	
Phone Number:	
E-mail Address:	
Balance:	
Date:	
PIN:	
Secret Question:	
Answer:	
Additional Important Information:	

Other — Account 1

Financial Institution:	
Account Number:	
Contact:	
Phone Number:	
E-mail Address:	
Balance:	
Date:	
PIN:	
Secret Question:	
Answer:	
Additional Important Information:	
Other – Account 2	
Financial Institution:	
Account Number:	
Contact:	
Phone Number:	
E-mail Address:	
Balance:	
Date:	
PIN:	
Secret Question:	
Answer:	
Additional Important Information:	

Anything that did not fit in a predetermined category: _____

_____

_____

_____

_____

Party Planning with an Unusual Twist

Whether you prefer a traditional and dignified ceremony, or an occasion that is a reflection of how you lived your life, the arrangements for the last event you will attend on Earth can be up to you. But you need to make the necessary arrangements, or direct others to do as you wish. *This is not a legally binding document; a lawyer will need to be consulted for the correct language and paperwork.*

Check all that apply (leave blank those things you do not want) and provide any details that are needed.

Your body:

☐ I want my body to be donated to medicine and used for the following purposes: _____

_____

☐ Release the final report, including all test results, to my executor/personal representative: _____

_____

☐ Conduct a post-mortem examination if the following circumstances occur: _____

_____

☐ Cremate my remains, and disposal of my ashes should be conducted as follows: _____

_____

☐ I request a burial to take place in this way: _____

_____

Your service:

☐ I want a memorial service without a casket.

☐ I want a funeral without a casket.

☐ Memorial service with a casket conducted in the following manner:

  ☐ Closed
  ☐ Open
  ☐ Funeral home/mortuary: _____
    Address: _____
    Phone: _____

☐ I would like a funeral service conducted in the following manner:

  Place of worship: _____

  Address: _____

  Phone: _____

  Presiding clergy: _____

  Soloist: _____

  Hymns: _____

  _____

  Musical selections: _____

  _____

  Musical instruments: _____

  _____

  Scripture, poem(s), and other materials to be included: _____

  _____

  _____

  Other instructions: _____

  _____

  _____

  _____

  _____

Memorial gifts should be suggested for the following: _____

_____

_____

Other information: _____

_____

_____

Signed: _____ Date: _____

Estate Plan Summary Sheet

There are many components that can go into an estate plan, but there are some basic documents that most people have. This is a brief inventory that can serve as a checklist for making sure you get the things done that you need to accomplish.

Use the blank lines to add other documents, such as a prenuptial agreement, that will affect your estate plan.

Estate Plan Components	Deadline	Done On	Notes
Estate Plan Summary Sheet			
Will			
Living Will			
Organ Donor Form/Card			
Durable Power of Attorney			
Medical Power of Attorney			
Guardians for Children			
Guardians for Others			

Life Insurance Policies			
Trust: For Children			
Trust: For Retirement			
Trust: For Charity _____			
Trust: For Charity _____			
Trust: Living _____			
Retirement: 401(k)/Pension			
_____			
_____			
_____			
_____			

Use the Notes sections as reminders for additional information that is needed before the next review; for example, "Get name of Peace Center lawyer" to make sure you have a contact for the charitable trust documents that might need to get to the organization.

Annual To-Do List

Once your estate plan is complete, this list will need to be customized to include each component.

Use the blank lines to add other documents, such as a prenuptial agreement, that will affect your estate plan.

Estate Plan Pieces	Meeting Date	Changes Needed
Estate Plan Summary Sheet		
Will		

Living Will		
Organ Donor Form/Card		
Durable Power of Attorney		
Medical Power of Attorney		
Guardians for Children		
Guardians for Others		
Life Insurance Policies		
Trust: _____		
Trust: _____		
Trust: _____		
Trust: _____		
Retirement: _____		
Retirement: _____		
_____		
_____		
_____		
_____		
_____		

APPENDIX B

New York Guardianship Court Forms

F.C.A. § 661;
S.C.P.A.§§ 1701 - 1704

Form 6-1
(Petition for Appointment
As Guardian of a Person Or
Permanent Guardian)
3/2009

....
Proceeding for the Appointment of a
Guardian of the Person or Permanent Guardian of

Docket No.
Family File No.
PETITION FOR
APPOINTMENT AS
❑Guardian of Person
❑Permanent Guardian

A Person Under the Age of 21
....

TO THE FAMILY COURT:

The Petitioner respectfully alleges to this Court that:
1. I am [specify relationship]:   of the person under the age of
21 who is the subject of this petition and I am submitting this petition in order to be appointed
[check applicable box]: ❑Guardian of the Person ❑Permanent Guardian.[1]

2. My name is [specify]:   and I live at [specify
name and complete address of residence]:[2]

3. The name, date of birth and residence of the person under the age of 21 who is the subject of this proceeding are as follows:

Name:

Date of Birth:

Complete address:[3]

---

[1] A "permanent guardian" may be appointed, pursuant to Family Court Act §661(b) and Surrogate's Court Procedure Act §1702(2), if the Court finds that it is in the best interests of a person under the age of 21, who has been committed to an authorized agency through termination of parental rights or surrender or whose birth parents or other persons entitled to notice of, or to consent to, adoption are deceased. Persons over the age of 18 must consent to such an appointment, which may last until the person reaches the age of 21.

[2] Unless the Court has ordered the address to be confidential on the ground that disclosure would pose an unreasonable health or safety risk. *See* Family Court Act §154-b; Form 21 (available at www.nycourts.gov).

[3] Unless the Court has ordered the address to be confidential on the ground that disclosure would pose an unreasonable health or safety risk. *See* Family Court Act §154-b; Form 21 (available at www.nycourts.gov).

4. The subject of this proceeding ☐is ☐is not a Native American child under the age of 18 who is subject to the *Indian Child Welfare Act of 1978* (25 U.S.C. §§1901-1963). If so, the following have been notified [check applicable box(es)]:

☐ parent/custodian [specify name and give notification date]:

☐ tribe/nation [specify name and give notification date]:

☐ United States Secretary of the Interior [give notification date]:

5. The name and relationship of person with whom the subject of this proceeding resides are as follows:

Person with whom subject resides [specify name]:

Relationship to subject:

Address [include street, city, village or town, county and state]:[4]

6. (Upon information and belief) The religion of the person who is the subject of this proceeding is

7. The names, relationship and post office addresses of the birth parents of the subject of the proceeding, the name and address of the person with whom the subject resides, if other than the parent(s), on whom process should issue; and such other persons concerning whom the court is required to have information, are as follows: [If either birth parent is dead or has surrendered or has had parental rights terminated (TPR) , so allege; if both parents are dead, indicate nearest adult next of kin]:

Relationship	Name	Complete Address	Deceased?	TPR?	Surrender?
Birth mother:					
Birth father:					
Person with whom the subject resides, if other than parents:					
Adult next of kin, if birth parents are dead:					
Other [specify]:[5]					

---

[4] Unless the Court has ordered the address to be confidential on the ground that disclosure would pose an unreasonable health or safety risk. *See* Family Court Act §154-b; Form 21 (available at www.nycourts.gov).

[5] Include Mental Hygiene Legal Services, if the subject of the proceeding is mentally retarded or developmentally disabled and has been admitted to a facility, and any person entitled to notice of or consent to the adoption of the subject of the proceeding.

8. a. Appointing me as the ◻guardian of the person ◻permanent guardian would be in [subject's name]:   best interests and would preserve his/her legal rights because [specify facts regarding the suitability, ability and commitment of the proposed guardian to assume full legal responsibility and raise him/her to adulthood]:

b. [Required where appointment of permanent guardian is requested, pursuant to Family Court Act §661(b) or S.C.P.A. §1702(2); delete if inapplicable]:
(i) [Check applicable box]:
❑ guardianship and custody have been committed to the following authorized agency [specify, include whether by surrender or termination of parental rights and attach certified copies of the orders terminating parental rights or approving the surrenders, as applicable]:

❑ both parents of the child, whose consent to or notice of an adoption would have been required, are deceased [attach death certificates].

(ii) The local social services district performed an assessment, as required by S.C.P.A. §1704(8), that recommended the following [specify and attach a copy of the assessment]:

9: [Applicable to cases in which child protective petition or permanency hearing report has been filed regarding the children and in which petitioner is a relative or other non-parent; delete if inapplicable]:
a. ◻ A child protective petition, Docket # [specify]:   , was filed in Family Court, [specify county]:   on [specify date]:   alleging that [specify names of respondents on that petition]:
neglected or abused the above-named child(ren). The petition resulted in [specify whether finding was made and, if so, the disposition; if the disposition has been adjourned pending a consolidated hearing with this petition, pursuant to F.C.A. §1055-b, so indicate and give next court date]:

b. ◻ A permanency report, Docket # [specify]:   , pursuant to Article 10-A of the Family Court Act, was filed in Family Court, [specify county]:   on [specify date]: indicating a permanency plan of guardianship of the child(ren) with Petitioner in this proceeding. The permanency hearing was adjourned to [specify date]:   pending a consolidated hearing with this petition, pursuant to F.C.A. §1089-a.

c. The child's birth mother ◻ has ◻ has not consented to the award of guardianship to the Petitioner. If not, the following extraordinary circumstances support Petitioner's standing to seek guardianship of the child(ren) [specify]:

d. The child's legally-established birth father ◻ has ◻ has not consented to the award of guardianship to the Petitioner. If not, the following extraordinary circumstances support Petitioner's standing to seek guardianship of the child(ren) [specify]:

e. The child has been living with the following foster parent(s)[specify]: since [specify date]:   The foster parent(s)
◻ has/have ◻ has/have not consented to the award of guardianship to the Petitioner. [If unaware whether they have consented, so state]:

f. The local department of social services [specify]:   in the related ◻ child abuse or neglect ◻ permanency proceeding ◻ has ◻ has not consented to the award of guardianship to the Petitioner. [If unaware whether they have consented, so state]:

g. The attorney for the child(ren) [specify]:   in the related ◻ child abuse or neglect ◻ permanency proceeding ◻ has ◻ has not consented to the award of guardianship to the Petitioner. [If unaware whether they have consented, so state]:

9. (Upon information and belief) No guardian pursuant to will or deed, or guardian of the person pursuant to Section 384 or 384-b of the Social Services Law, has been previously appointed for the subject of this proceeding, except [specify]:

10. Upon information and belief, [Check all applicable box(es)]:

a.   ☐ I have never been the subject of an indicated report, as such term is defined in of the Social Services Law §412, that has been filed with the statewide register of child abuse and maltreatment pursuant Social Services Law §422.

☐ I was the subject of an indicated report, as defined in of the Social Services Law §412, that was filed with the statewide register of child abuse and maltreatment pursuant Social Services Law §422. [Specify the date of the report, determination of whether "indicated" or "unfounded," status and circumstances to the extent known]:

____   ☐ I am the subject of a report, as defined in of the Social Services Law §412, filed with the statewide register of child abuse and maltreatment pursuant Social Services Law §422, that remains under investigation. [Specify the date of the report, status and circumstances to the extent known]:

____   b.   ☐ I have never been the subject of, or the respondent in, a child protective proceeding pursuant to Article Ten of the Family Court Act.

☐ I have been the subject of, or the respondent in, a child protective proceeding pursuant to Article Ten of the Family Court Act. [Specify whether the proceeding resulted in an order finding that a child or children was/were abused or neglected, indicate whether the subject of this proceeding was found to be abused or neglected and provide the date and status of the proceeding to the extent known]:

c.   ☐ I have never been the subject of an Order of Protection or Temporary Order of Protection in any criminal, matrimonial or Family Court proceeding(s).

☐ I have been the subject of an Order of Protection or Temporary Order of Protection in a criminal, matrimonial or Family Court proceeding(s) as follows [specify the court, docket or index number, whether I was protected or restrained by the order, date of order, expiration date of order, next court date and status of case to the extent known]:

11.   Upon information and belief,[check applicable box(es)]:

a. The following adults who are age 18 or older live in my home:

Name   Relationship, if any, to subject of proceeding   Date of Birth

b.   ☐ None of the adults 18 or older living in my home has ever been the subject of any indicated reports, as defined in of the Social Services Law §412, that were filed with the statewide register of child abuse and maltreatment pursuant Social Services Law §422.

☐ The following adults 18 or older living in my home have been the subjects of indicated reports, as defined in of the Social Services Law §412, that were filed with the statewide register of child abuse and maltreatment pursuant Social Services Law §422. [Specify the name(s) of the adults, date(s) of the report(s), whether the subject of this proceeding was the subject of the report(s), status and circumstances to the extent known]:

____   ☐ The following adults 18 or older living in my home are the subjects of reports, as defined in of the Social Services Law §412, filed with the statewide register of child abuse and maltreatment pursuant Social Services Law §422, that remain under investigation [Specify the name(s) of the adults, whether the subject of this proceeding is the subject of the report(s), date(s) of the report(s), status and circumstances to the extent known]:

c. ☐ None of the adults 18 or older living in my home has ever been the subjects of, or the respondents in, child protective proceedings pursuant to Article Ten of the Family Court Act.
☐ the following adults 18 or older living in my home have been the subjects of, or the respondents in, child protective proceedings pursuant to Article Ten of the Family Court Act, as follows [Specify the names of the adults, whether the proceedings have resulted in orders finding that the child is an abused or neglected child, whether the subject of this proceeding was a subject of those proceedings and the date and status of the proceedings to the extent known]:

d. ☐ None of the adults 18 or older living in my home has ever been the subjects of an Order of Protection or Temporary Order of Protection in any criminal, matrimonial or Family Court proceeding(s).
☐ the following adults 18 or older living in my home have been the subjects of Orders of Protection or Temporary Orders of Protection in criminal, matrimonial or Family Court proceeding(s), as follows [specify the names of the adults, whether the adults are or were restrained or protected by the order(s), court, docket or index number, date of order, expiration date of order, next court date and status of cases to the extent known]:

12. The birth parent(s) of the child [specify]:
although living, should not be appointed guardian of the person of the child because:

13. a. [Applicable where the subject of the proceeding is 18 years of age or older; delete if inapplicable]: The person who is the subject of this proceeding is over the age of 18 and has consented to the appointment of the guardian, a copy of which is attached.
b. [Applicable where the child is over 14 years of age but less than 18; delete if inapplicable]: The child, who is over the age of 14, has expressed a preference for the appointment of the guardian, a copy of which is attached.

14. There are no persons interested in this proceeding other than those mentioned above.

15. No prior application has been made to any court, including a Native- American tribunal, for the relief requested herein (except [specify]:   ).

WHEREFORE, Petitioner requests that an order be entered appointing me to be the ☐guardian of the person ☐permanent guardian of [specify]:
until the child reaches the age of ☐18 ☐21 upon his/her consent, and that letters of guardianship issue.

Dated:
_____
Signature of Petitioner

_____
Print or type name

_____   _____
Signature of Attorney, if any

_____   _____
Attorney's Name (Print or Type)

_____   _____
Attorney's Address and Telephone Number

_____VERIFICATION_____

STATE OF NEW YORK   )
)ss.:
COUNTY OF   )
                    ,being duly sworn, says that (s)he is the Petitioner in the above-named proceeding and that the foregoing petition is true to (his)(her) own knowledge, except as to matters therein stated to be alleged on information and belief and as to those matters (s)he believes it to be true.

Sworn to before me this
day of   .

_____
Petitioner

_____
(Deputy)Clerk of the Court
   Notary Public

F.C.A;§. 661
S.C.P.A.§§ 1704,1726

Form 6-8
(Petition for Appointment
of Standby Guardian)
1/2001

FAMILY COURT OF THE STATE OF NEW YORK
COUNTY OF
....

Proceeding for the Appointment of a
Standby Guardian of the Person

Docket No.

of

PETITION
(Appointment of
Standby Guardian)

_____, a Minor
....

TO THE FAMILY COURT:

The Petitioner respectfully alleges to this Court that:

1. The name and domicile of the Petitioner and relationship of the Petitioner to the child who is the subject of this proceeding, are as follows:

Name:
Relationship to child [check applicable box]:
  ❐ mother   ❐ father   ❐ guardian   ❐ legal custodian   ❐ primary caretaker
Address [Include street, city, village or town, county and state]:

2. The name, date of birth and domicile of the child who is the subject of this proceeding are as follows:
  Name:
  Date of Birth:
  Address: [Including street, city, village or town, county and state]

3. The subject child (is)(is not) a Native American child subject to the Indian Child Welfare Act of 1978 (25 U.S.C. §§ 1901-1963).

4.The residence of the child and name and relationship of the person(s) with whom the child resides are as follows:
  Person with whom child resides [specify name]:
  Relationship to child [check applicable box]:
    ❐ mother   ❐ father   ❐ guardian   ❐ legal custodian   ❐ primary caretaker
  Address [Include street, city, village or town, county and state]:

5. This petition seeks appointment of a Standby Guardian of the person of the child who is the subject of this proceeding, to become effective upon the petitioner's (incapacity) (death) (incapacity or death, whichever occurs first).[1]

6. On information and belief, petitioner suffers from a progressively chronic or fatal illness. The source of information and basis for belief are:

7. The religion of the child is

8. The names, relationship and post office addresses of the child's parent(s), the name and address of the person(s) with whom the child resides, if other than the parent(s), to whom process should issue; and such other persons concerning whom the court is required to have information, are as follows:
(If a parent is deceased, so allege)

Relationship	Name	Post Office Address
Mother:		

Father:

Person with whom
Child resides, if
other than parents:

Other:[2]

     9. To protect and preserve the legal rights of the child, it is necessary that some proper person be duly appointed the Standby Guardian of (his)(her) person, because:

     10. (Upon information and belief) No Guardian pursuant to Section 383-c, 384 or 384-b of the Social Services Law, or Standby Guardian pursuant to section 1726 of the Surrogate's Court Procedure Act, has been previously appointed for the child except [specify]:

     11. (a). Petitioner (has)(does not have) knowledge that the person nominated to be a

---

[1] S.C.P.A. Section 1726(3)(I); delete inapplicable provisions.

[2]Include Mental Hygiene Legal Services if child is a mentally retarded or developmentally disabled person admitted to a facility.

standby guardian herein is the subject of an indicated report, as such term is defined in Section 412 of the Social Services Law, filed with the statewide register of child abuse and maltreatment pursuant to Title Six of Article Six of the Social Services Law. If so, specify date, status and circumstances to the extent known:

     (b). Petitioner (has)(does not have) knowledge that the person nominated to be a standby guardian] herein is the subject of or the respondent in a child protective proceeding commenced under Article Ten of the Family Court Act. If so, specify whether proceeding resulted in an order finding that the child is an abused or neglected child, date and status to the extent known:

     (c). Petitioner (has)(does not have) knowledge that an Order of Protection or Temporary Order of Protection (has)(has not) been issued against the person nominated to be a guardian herein in any criminal, matrimonial or Family Court proceeding(s). If such an order has been issued, specify the court, docket or index number, date of order, expiration date or order, next court date and status of case to the extent known:

     12 (a). The following adults aged 18 or older reside with the proposed guardian:

Name	Relationship, if any, to Child	Date of Birth

     (b). Upon information and belief, (none of the above adults) (the following adult(s)[specify]:) (is)(are) the subject of an indicated report, as such term is defined in Section 412 of the Social Services Law, filed with the statewide register of child abuse and maltreatment pursuant to Title Six of Article Six of the Social Services Law. If so, specify date, status and circumstances to the extent known:

     (c). Upon information and belief, (none of the above adults) (the following adult(s)[specify]:) (has) (have) been the subject of or the respondent in a child protective proceeding commenced under Article 10 of the Family Court Act. If so, specify whether proceeding resulted in an order finding that the child is an abused or neglected child, date and status to the extent known:

(d). Upon information and belief, an Order of Protection or Temporary Order of Protection (has)(has not) been issued against any of the above adults in any criminal, matrimonial or Family Court proceeding(s). If such an order has been issued, specify the adult against whom the order was issued, the court that issued the order, docket number, date of order, expiration date of order, next court date and status of case to the extent known:

13.   , residing at   , whose standby guardian herein is the subject of an indicated report, as such term is defined in Section 412 of the Social Services Law, filed with the statewide register of child abuse and maltreatment pursuant to Title Six of Article Six of the Social Services Law. If so, specify date, status and circumstances to the extent known:

(b). Petitioner (has)(does not have) knowledge that the person nominated to be a standby guardian] herein is the subject of or the respondent in a child protective proceeding commenced under Article Ten of the Family Court Act. If so, specify whether proceeding resulted in an order finding that the child is an abused or neglected child, date and status to the extent known:

(c). Petitioner (has)(does not have) knowledge that an Order of Protection or Temporary Order of Protection (has)(has not) been issued against the person nominated to be a guardian herein in any criminal, matrimonial or Family Court proceeding(s). If such an order has been issued, specify the court, docket or index number, date of order, expiration date or order, next court date and status of case to the extent known:

12 (a). The following adults aged 18 or older reside with the proposed guardian:

Name	Relationship, if any, to Child	Date of Birth

(b). Upon information and belief, (none of the above adults) (the following adult(s)[specify]:) (is)(are) the subject of an indicated report, as such term is defined in Section 412 of the Social Services Law, filed with the statewide register of child abuse and maltreatment pursuant to Title Six of Article Six of the Social Services Law. If so, specify date, status and circumstances to the extent known:

(c). Upon information and belief, (none of the above adults) (the following adult(s)[specify]:) (has) (have) been the subject of or the respondent in a child protective proceeding commenced under Article 10 of the Family Court Act. If so, specify whether proceeding resulted in an order finding that the child is an abused or neglected child, date and status to the extent known:

(d). Upon information and belief, an Order of Protection or Temporary Order of Protection (has)(has not) been issued against any of the above adults in any criminal, matrimonial or Family Court proceeding(s). If such an order has been issued, specify the adult against whom the order was issued, the court that issued the order, docket number, date of order, expiration date of order, next court date and status of case to the extent known:

13.   , residing at   , whose religion is   would be a suitable and proper person to be appointed Standby Guardian of the person of the Child, in that:

14. Attached hereto is the consent of the proposed Standby Guardian to being appointed Standby Guardian of the person of the child.

(15. [Delete if inapplicable]: The parent(s) of the child, although living, should not be appointed Standby Guardian of the person of the child because:
).

16. There are no persons interested in this proceeding other than those here in above mentioned.

17. No prior application has been made to any court for the relief herein requested.

WHEREFORE, Petitioner respectfully requests that an order be entered appointing   [specify]: as Standby Guardian of the person of the child upon Petitioner's death (or incapacity, whichever occurs first). [Delete if inapplicable. *See* S.C.P.A. §1726(3)].

Dated:

_____
Signature of Petitioner

_____
Print or type name

_____
Signature of Attorney, if any

_____
Attorney's Name (Print or Type)

_____

_____
Attorney's Address and Telephone Number

VERIFICATION

STATE OF NEW YORK   )
) ss.:
COUNTY OF   )
, being duly sworn, says that b(s)he is the Petitioner in the above-named proceeding and that the foregoing petition is true to (his)(her) own knowledge, except as to matters therein stated to be alleged on information and belief and as to those matters (s)he believes it to be true.

_____
Petitioner

Sworn to before me this

    day of   ,   .

_____
(Deputy) Clerk of the court
        Notary Public

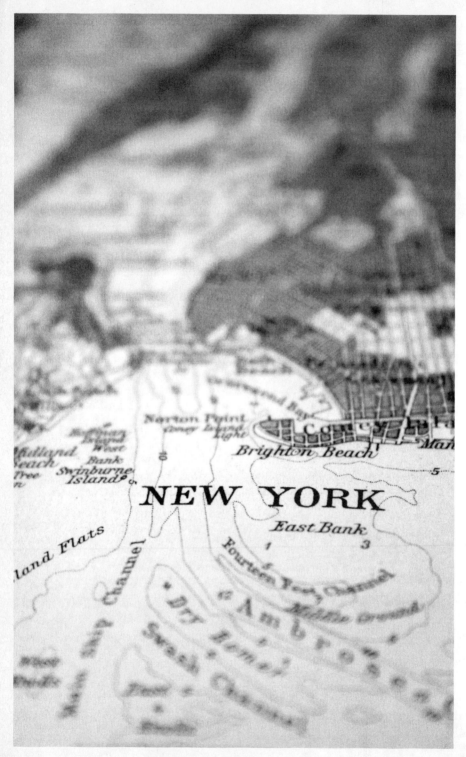

APPENDIX C
New York's Prudent Investor Act

NY Code section EPT 11-2.3

(a) Prudent investor rule.

A trustee has a duty to invest and manage property held in a fiduciary capacity in accordance with the prudent investor standard defined by this section, except as otherwise provided by the express terms and provisions of a governing instrument within the limitations set forth by section 11-1.7 of this chapter. This section shall apply to any investment made or held on or after January first, nineteen hundred ninety-five by a trustee.

(b) Prudent investor standard.

(1) The prudent investor rule requires a standard of conduct, not outcome or performance. Compliance with the prudent investor rule is determined in light of facts and circumstances prevailing at the time of the decision or action of a trustee. A trustee is not liable to a beneficiary to the extent that the trustee acted in substantial compliance with the prudent investor standard or in reasonable reliance on the express terms and provisions of the governing instrument.

(2) A trustee shall exercise reasonable care, skill and caution to make and implement investment and management decisions as a prudent inves-

tor would for the entire portfolio, taking into account the purposes and terms and provisions of the governing instrument.

(3) The prudent investor standard requires a trustee:

(A) to pursue an overall investment strategy to enable the trustee to make appropriate present and future distributions to or for the benefit of the beneficiaries under the governing instrument, in accordance with risk and return objectives reasonably suited to the entire portfolio;

(B) to consider, to the extent relevant to the decision or action, the size of the portfolio, the nature and estimated duration of the fiduciary relationship, the liquidity and distribution requirements of the governing instrument, general economic conditions, the possible effect of inflation or deflation, the expected tax consequences of investment decisions or strategies and of distributions of income and principal, the role that each investment or course of action plays within the overall portfolio, the expected total return of the portfolio (including both income and appreciation of capital), and the needs of beneficiaries (to the extent reasonably known to the trustee) for present and future distributions authorized or required by the governing instrument;

(C) to diversify assets unless the trustee reasonablydetermines that it is in the interests of the beneficiaries not to diversify, taking into account the purposes and terms and provisions of the governing instrument; and

(D) within a reasonable time after the creation of the fiduciary relationship, to determine whether to retain or dispose of initial assets.

(4) The prudent investor standard authorizes a trustee:

(A) to invest in any type of investment consistent with the requirements of this paragraph, since no particular investment is inherently prudent or imprudent for purposes of the prudent investor standard;

(B) to consider related trusts, the income and resources of beneficiaries to the extent reasonably known to the trustee, and also an asset's special relationship or value to some or all of the beneficiaries if consistent with the trustee's duty of impartiality;

(C) to delegate investment and management functions if consistent with the duty to exercise skill, including special investment skills; and

(D) to incur costs only to the extent they are appropriate and reasonable in relation to the purposes of the governing instrument, the ssets held by the trustee and the skills of the trustee.

(5) Trustee's power to adjust.

(A) Where the rules in article 11-A apply to a trust and the terms of the trust describe the amount that may or must be distributed to a beneficiary by referring to the trust's income, the prudent investor standard also authorizes the trustee to adjust between principal and income to the extent the trustee considers advisable to enable the trustee to make appropriate present and future distributions in accordance with clause (b)(3)(A) if the trustee determines, in light of its investment decisions, the consideration factors incorporated in clause (b)(5)(B), and the accounting income expected to be produced by applying the rules in article 11-A, that such an adjustment would be fair and reasonable to all of the beneficiaries.

(B) In deciding whether and to what extent to exercise the power conferred by clause (b)(5)(A), a trustee may consider, in addition to the factors stated in clauses (b)(3)(B) and (b)(4)(B), the following factors to the extent relevant:

(i) the intent of the settlor, as expressed in the governing instrument; the assets held in the trust; the extent to which they consist of financial assets, interest in closely held enterprises, tangible and intangible personal property, or real property; the extent to which an asset is used by a beneficiary; and whether an asset was purchased by the trustee or received from the settlor;

(ii) the net amount allocated to income under article 11-A and the increase or decrease in the value of the principal assets, which the trustee may estimate as to assets for which market values are not readily available; and

(iii) whether and to what extent the terms of the trust give the trustee the power to invade principal or accumulate income or prohibit the trustee from invading principal or accumulating income, and the extent to which the trustee has exercised a power from time to time to invade principal or accumulate income.

(C) A trustee may not make an adjustment:

(i) with respect to a charitable remainder unitrust described in section 664 of the United States internal revenue code of 1986;

(ii) that changes the amount payable to a beneficiary as a fixed annuity or a fixed fraction of the value of the trust's assets;

(iii) from any amount that is permanently set aside for charitable purposes under a will or the terms of a trust unless the income therefrom is also permanently devoted to charitable purposes;

(iv) if possessing or exercising the power to make an djustment causes an individual to be treated as the owner of all or part of the trust for income tax purposes, and the individual would not be treated as the owner if the trustee did not possess the power to make an adjustment;

(v) if possessing or exercising the power to make an adjustment causes all or part of the trust assets to be included for estate tax purposes in the estate of an individual who has the power to remove a trustee or appoint a trustee, or both, and the assets would not be included in the estate of the individual if the trustee did not possess the power to make an adjustment;

(vi) If the trustee is a current beneficiary or a presumptive remainderman of the trust;

(vii) if the trustee is not a current beneficiary or a presumptive remainderman, but the adjustment would benefit the trustee directly or indirectly (which, however, shall not include the possible effect on a trustee's commission); or

(viii) if the trust is an irrevocable lifetime trust which provides income to be paid for life to the grantor, and possessing or exercising the power to make an adjustment would cause any public benefit program to consider the adjusted principal or income to be an available resource or available income and the principal or income or both would in each case not be considered as an available resource or income if the trustee did not possess the power to make an adjustment;

(D) An adjustment otherwise prohibited by items (b)(5)(C)(i) through (viii) may be made if the terms of the trust, by express reference to this section, provide otherwise. If item (b)(5)(C) (iv), (v), (vi) or (vii) applies to a trustee and there is more than one trustee, the trustee or trustees to whom the provision does not apply may make the adjustment unless the exercise of the power by the remaining trustee or trustees is prohibited by the terms of the trust. If there is no trustee qualified to make the adjustment, it may be made if so directed by the court upon application of the trustee or of an interested party.

(E) A trustee may release the entire power conferred by clause (b)(5)(A) or may release only the power to adjust from income to principal or the power to adjust from principal to income if the trustee is uncertain about whether possessing or exercising the power will cause a result described in items (b)(5)(C)(i) through (vi) or (b)(5)(C)(viii) or if the trustee determines that possessing or exercising the power will or may deprive the trust of a tax benefit or impose a tax burden not described in clause (b)(5)(C). The release may be permanent or for a specified period, including a period measured by the life of an individual.

(F) Terms of a trust that limit the power of a trustee to make an adjustment between principal and income are not contrary to this section unless it is clear from the terms of the trust that the terms are intended to deny the trustee the power of adjustment conferred by clause (b)(5)(A).

(6) Special investment skills.

For a bank, trust company or paid professional investment advisor (whether or not registered under any federal securities or investment law) which serves as a trustee, and any other trustee representing that such trustee has special investment skills, the exercise of skill contemplated by the prudent investor standard shall require the trustee to exercise such diligence in investing and managing assets as would customarily be exercised by prudent investors of discretion and intelligence having special investment skills.

(c) Delegation of investment or management functions.

(1) Delegation of an investment or management function requires a trustee to exercise care, skill and caution in:

(A) selecting a delegee suitable to exercise the delegated function, taking into account the nature and value of the assets subject to such delegation and the expertise of the delegee;

(B) establishing the scope and terms of the delegation consistent with the purposes of the governing instrument;

(C) periodically reviewing the delegee's exercise of the delegated function and compliance with the scope and terms of the delegation; and

(D) controlling the overall cost by reason of the delegation.

(2) The delegee has a duty to the trustee and to the trust to comply with the scope and terms of the delegation and to exercise the delegated function with reasonable care, skill and caution. An attempted exoneration of the delegee from liability for failure to meet such duty is contrary to public policy and void.

(3) By accepting the delegation of a trustee's function from the trustee of a trust that is subject to the law of New York, the delegee submits to the jurisdiction of the courts of New York even if a delegation agreement provides otherwise, and the delegee may be made a party to any proceeding in such courts that places in issuethe decisions or actions of the delegee.

(d) Investment in securities of related investment companies.

A trustee holding funds for investment may invest the same in securities of any management type investment company or trust registered pursuant to the federal investment company act of nineteen hundred forty, as amended, notwithstanding that the trustee or an affiliate of the trustee acts as investment advisor, custodian, transfer agent, registrar, sponsor, distributor, manager or provides other services to the investment company or trust. Unless the will, lifetime trust or order appointing the trustee provides otherwise, the trustee shall elect annually either (i) to receive or have its affiliate receive compensation for providing such services to such investment company or trust for the portion of the trust invested in such investment company or trust or (ii) to take annual corporate trustees' commissions with respect to such portion.

(e) As used in this section.

(1) the term "trustee" includes a personal representative, trustee, guardian, donee of a power during minority, guardian under article eighty-one of the mental hygiene law, committee of the property of an incompetent person, and conservator of the property of a conservatee;

(2) the term "trust" includes any fiduciary entity with property owned by a trustee as defined in this section;

(3) the term "governing instrument" includes a court order; and

(4) the term "portfolio" includes all property of every kind and character held by a trustee as defined in this section.

APPENDIX D
Glossary of Terms

#

401(k) Plan – Named after the IRS code number defining this kind of plan, this retirement savings plan allows contributions to be made automatically by your employer via deductions from your paycheck, pre-tax. This plan only applies to for-profit businesses.

403(b) Plan – This is the 401(k) equivalent for not-for-profit entities and is named after the IRS code number defining this kind of retirement savings plan. It allows contributions to be made automatically by your employer via deductions from your paycheck, pre-tax.

A

Adeemed – The status given to a will if property is missing from your estate that is specifically named in the will.

Ademption Statute – State law governing the distribution of property in an estate if items are missing or adeemed.

Administrator – If you die without a will, the court appoints an individual, regularly a spouse or child, who will serve in the same capacity as an executor. That person will handle all the estate paperwork, prepare a list of assets, deal with likely heirs, handle claims from creditors, make payments on outstanding debt, and handle other estate-related matters.

Annuity – A retirement investment account that you create by contributing a specific amount of money over a predetermined period of time; there will be a fixed rate of return for a number of years.

▶ **Variable Annuity** – A retirement investment account that you create by contributing a specific amount of money over a predetermined period of time; the funds are invested in the stock market, so the return depends on how well or poorly the economy does.

Antilapse – The status of a will if a beneficiary in your will dies before you do.

Antilapse Statute – State law that dictates the state will intervene if the property in a will exists, but the beneficiary is no longer alive, and no contingent beneficiary is named.

Appointment Clause – A giving clause in your will that identifies the person who will manage your estate.

Asset – Anything a person owns or is owed; this can be money, real estate, investments, or any other tangible property.

Automobile Insurance – The exchange of premiums for a guaranteed payment to cover the damage or loss of a motor vehicle. Medical and liability coverage can also be included.

B

Bargain Sale – The sale of a piece of property to a charity at a rate that is below the fair market value. The difference between the amount paid and actual value is the amount of the gift.

Beneficiary – The individual(s) or group(s) who will receive the property in a will or trust. This can be a single person (a nephew), a group of people (all grandchildren), one group (Stray Cat Rescue, Inc.), several groups (all community councils in your city), or a combination of any of these.

Beneficial Title, or Equitable Title – The right of a person or institution to take possession of or benefit from the property in a trust.

Bequest – A legacy or gift given by a person to another person or entity through a last will and testament after the giver dies.

Burial Trust – Provides the funds necessary to cover the cost of your burial (or cremation) arrangements; this can be a revocable trust, but after your death, it becomes irrevocable, and the trust cannot be used for anything else.

Bypass Trust – This trust will transfer property to someone other than your spouse, such as a child or grandchild, but allows him or her to still benefit from the property in the trust.

C

Certified Public Accountant (CPA) – A person who has gone through professional training and meets state requirements for both education and work experience, passed a national accounting exam, and met other licensing requirements to perform the tasks of accounting such as performing audits, preparing tax returns, and giving advice to clients — individuals or businesses — on financial matters. Accountants can also specialize in various aspects of financial estate matters such as trusts, annuities, and estate tax law. But they also serve as estate-planning specialists who can help you consider all financial decisions.

Charitable Trust – A method for giving charitable institutions gifts, including regular support on a time-release basis, that are tax-free for the donor.

Charitable Remainder Trust – Gives gifts of interest income that are paid to specific beneficiaries, such as the charity or a spouse, for a specific period of time; at the end of that time period, the charity receives whatever is left in the trust.

Charitable Lead Trust – Also known as a front trust; gives the charity a specific gift before all other beneficiaries receive anything.

Clauses – The sections in your will that organize the information in a specific order.

Coach – These trained professionals specialize in offering financial, professional, and personal guidance to help you identify and manage monetary, career, and personal goals. There are certification courses for various forms of coaching, but there are no national standards, and formal training is not required to present oneself as a coach.

Codicil – A separate legal document that adds provisions to your existing will.

Cost-of-Living Adjustment – Some plans have a variable that will allow for annual increases in the payments made to the employee to help cover the cost of rising prices. Not all plans have this feature.

Crummey Trust – An extremely complicated trust normally set up in conjunction with an irrevocable life insurance trust to make the payments for a life insurance policy; this is the kind of trust that requires an estate-planning attorney.

Custodian Account – This account for minor children, which can be in the form of a trust, allows you to deposit money or property in an account set up by a bank or brokerage firm. You can name yourself as the custodian, or trustee, of the account while you are alive and then name a successor to take over those responsibilities after you die.

▶ **Uniform Transfer for Minors Act (UTMA)** – This is the most current federal regulation that defines and allows an account, or trust, to be set up for minor children; if a state adopted this regulation, it served to repeal their UGMA statute. New York has adopted the UTMA.

▶ **Uniform Gift to Minors Act (UGMA)** –This is the first federal regulation that defined and allows an account, or trust, to be set up for minor children; some states still have this form of the law on their books.

D

Decedent – A person who has died.

Disability Insurance – A disability insurance policy will make payments to you to cover living expenses and replace your lost income as a result of your inability to hold a job.

▶ **Short-term disability** provides benefits for about three months; some plans go a little longer, but only for a short period of time.

▶ **Long-term disability** can provide benefits for years but does eventually end, frequently at age 65 when you become eligible for social security.

Disclaimer – A refusal of a beneficiary to accept the gift given; recognized by both federal and state authorities if given in writing by a specific deadline, typically nine months after the donor's death.

Discretionary Trust – Gives a trustee the ability to distribute income and property to a variety of beneficiaries; he or she also has the option to control the distributions to a single beneficiary as he or she decides is appropriate.

Distribution – This is the disbursement or payment of property from an account to a beneficiary; it could be in the form of a check or some other monetary payment, or the transfer of a title into the name of the beneficiary.

Distribution Provisions – Any clause that identifies to whom the income will be given and the frequency of those distributions, such as payments made every April 15 to the IRS.

DNR – "Do not resuscitate," an advanced medical directive that expresses your wish to not be resuscitated or revived if you appear to have died.

Donee – The person or institution receiving a gift.

Donor – The person who gives a gift or bequest.

Dumpster Diving – A slang term used to describe the act of digging through trash to find bills, bank statements, or other documents with account information or any personal information that might be useful to an identity thief; this is not considered an act of theft because the U.S. Supreme Court ruled that anything left out for trash collection is in the public domain.

Durable Power of Attorney – Allows an authorized person to act on behalf of the grantor of that power of attorney.

Dynasty Trust – Also known as a wealth trust; can last for several generations or be set up to never end. This kind of trust helps people with a vast amount of wealth control the distribution of that money and property over a long period of time.

E

Educational Trust – This is a kind of protective trust that sets aside money specifically for education-related expenses, such as tuition or training fees, books, or supplies. These trusts include provisions to stop payments if the student drops out of school or flunks numerous classes.

Ending Clauses – These include the legalities to meet statutory requirements so that your will is legal and valid, which include (but are not limited to) your signature, date, location of the signing, and witnesses.

Estate Planning – Creating a set of instructions about what should be done with your things — money, possessions, investments, collectibles, or anything you own — before and after you die.

Estate Tax – Referred to as the "death tax" by Congress, this is the federal tax on the property in your estate after you die.

Executor – Also called a personal representative, this is the individual who handles the property you are leaving behind. If you die without a will, the court appoints an administrator, frequently a spouse or child.

Exemption – This is a specific amount of money that will not be affected by estate taxes. Federal taxes and states with an estate tax often set an amount, such as $1 million, that is "tax-free," and then taxes are due on $1.01 million and beyond.

F

Family Consent – Also known as a health surrogate, this is a family member designated by state law who will make medical decisions for you when you cannot do it for yourself. These laws follow a specific order of kinship for who makes a decision — if you are married, your spouse, not your sister, will be your surrogate.

Family Trust – A legal arrangement that involves the transfer of property from the original owner to a family member for the purpose of holding and maintaining the property until the beneficiary takes ownership.

Fiduciary Powers Clause – A giving clause in your will that includes language giving your executor the power to serve as your executor, including any duties that go beyond the basic requirements in your state regulations.

Financial Planner – Certified Financial Planners® (CFP®), Chartered Financial Analyst (CFA), and some without initials are individuals who analyze the overall financial situation of an individual and then develop a comprehensive plan, in conjunction with the individual, that will attempt to meet his or her financial goals and objectives. Planners who are certified have followed a specific course of education or training classes, and some go on to develop expertise in specific areas such as estate or retirement planning.

Funding a Trust – The placement of property in a trust; that same property will be called "trust principal" once it is under the auspices of the trust agreement.

G

Generation Skipping Tax Transfer (GSTT) – This is a federal tax levied on property transferred to a person one or more generations removed from the donor.

Generation Skipping Transfer Trust – A tax-saving trust that is designed to benefit multiple generations after you are gone.

Gift Tax – A federal tax levied against any property you give to another person or institution during a fiscal year; it can be in cash or the transfer of property, such as real estate or jewelry.

Giving Clauses – Explain what property goes to which person and under what circumstances. These can be as broad or explicit as you want. Real property clauses are statements that match up property with a person. Personal property clauses are used when you want to be explicit in your instructions. A residuary clause addresses the "leftovers" in your estate that you do not single out in a clause; this clause is essential for any kind of will to make sure that anything you forget or acquire since the will was prepared can be distributed. Making one or two beneficiaries is a good idea to keep your assets out of the hands of the courts.

Grantor-Retained Trusts – These are irrevocable, non-charitable trusts, which means they are set up in a way that is similar to a charitable trust, but the beneficiary is not a charity. There are three common types:

▶ **GRAT** – A grantor-retained annuity trust gives a fixed amount of money at predetermined times, often at regularly scheduled intervals.

▶ **GRIT** – A grantor-retained incomes trust designates specific people to receive certain property, such as stocks or a house, but the income or use of the property stays with you until your death.

▶ **GRUT** – A grantor-retained unit trust pays a specific percentage to the beneficiary.

Gross Estate – The value of all property owned by the deceased person on the date of that person's death; this is what gets taxed.

Guardian – The person legally appointed to be responsible for the needs of minor children until they reach a legal age; also, any adult who can be legally appointed to manage the affairs of an incompetent or infirm adult of any age.

Guardianship Clause – The appointment of a guardian for minor children (under the age of 18); a successor guardian should also be named as a backup.

H

Health Care Power of Attorney – Also known as medical power of attorney, this is the designation of a person who makes medical decisions for you when you cannot do it for yourself.

Heir – The legal title of a person who inherits property from an estate that does not have a will, or is intestate; beneficiaries are those who receive an inheritance by being named in a legal document such as a will or trust.

Homeowner's Insurance – The exchange of premiums for a guaranteed payment to cover the loss of a house and other personal property in the residence. Other coverage can also be included, such as personal liability.

Homestead Exemption Statute – State law that protects a family home from being sold to pay off creditors if there is not enough money in an estate to cover outstanding debt.

I

Individual Retirement Arrangement (IRA) – An investment account that you set up for yourself for retirement savings. There is a limit to the contributions you can make annually. There is a tax deduction for making these contributions every year, so technically they are tax-free contributions.

► **Roth IRA** – Named after its primary legislative sponsor, Senator William Roth of Delaware. Contributions to this IRA are also tax-deductible in the year they are made, and taxes are paid when the money is withdrawn. The difference here is that the interest earned while the money is invested will be tax-free if you own the Roth IRA for at least five years.

Inheritance Tax – A state tax levied on the property received by a beneficiary.

Insurance – A method of protecting valuables in the form of a policy in which premiums are paid over time to guarantee a specific payment for a specific purpose by the company accepting the premiums. Those valuables can be property, such as your home, car, or jewelry; a person; the ability to work and care for yourself; life; health care; and long-term care.

Insurance Agent – An individual who is authorized by an insurance company to represent that company when dealing with an applicant for insurance, be it a medical, disability, dental, or long-term care policy. An agent can help you with your policy purchase by assessing the kind and amount of insurance you need and can afford.

Intestate – To die without a will.

Inter Vivos Trust – A trust that is set up and takes effect during your lifetime, before your death.

Irrevocable – A trust that cannot be changed, no matter what.

J

Joint Will – This is one legal document for any two people, such as you and your spouse. The problem with this kind of will is that it is irrevocable, which means it cannot be changed after one of the two parties dies. The reason is that all decisions must be made by both people. A lawyer can tell you when this kind of will is a good idea, but most suggest separate wills to avoid complications.

Joint-with-Survivor Pension – When an employee dies, his or her benefits will be paid to his or her spouse for the remainder of the spouse's life. If the spouse waives that right, then the employee's pension payments will be larger (no need to set aside extra money for future payments), and the pension payments end when the employee dies.

K

Keogh Plan – Pronounced "key-oh," this is a qualified retirement plan for sole proprietors and partners but can also be used by employees. The restrictions, distributions, and other details are similar to a defined contribution plan or defined benefit plan.

"Kiddie Tax" – The nickname used to describe an income tax applied to money that minors did not earn through employment, also called unearned income. The special laws passed in 1996 were created to close a loophole that allowed parents to give their children a large gift as a way to pay a lower tax on the interest earned; the child tax rate was significantly lower than the adult rate.

L

Lawyer – An individual who has completed a course of study in the law and passed a state certification exam that authorizes him or her to practice law and/or give legal advice. Also called attorneys, these people can specialize in specific aspects of estate planning, such as wills, trusts, or probate court, or they might have a more broad focus, such as estate planning or tax law.

Legal Title – Legal position that gives the trustee ownership of the property in a trust for the duration of the trustee's responsibility.

Liability – A debt or an obligation to pay money to another person or institution.

Life Insurance – A financial arrangement in which an individual makes payments on a policy that guarantees the payment of a specific amount of money to a beneficiary upon the death of the person who is covered by the policy.

Living Trust – Created while you are still alive, this trust allows you to be the grantor, trustee, and beneficiary if you choose; this is considered a "will substitute" as a way to avoid probate.

Living Will – Also known as a medical directive, this is a legal document in which you spell out the decisions you have made about your medical care while you are still alive.

Long-term Care Insurance – This insurance provides payments to cover the cost of medical care. In-home nursing or nursing-home fees are examples of what might be covered.

M

Marital Dedication Trust – Puts property into a trust that is exclusively for your spouse, who decides what happens to the property after your death.

Medical Insurance – Frequently referred to as "health" insurance by those who sell it, the insurance that covers medical costs when you are sick and trying to cure an illness, injured, pregnant, and for regular checkups.

Medicaid – State-run medical insurance plan that is supported by federal funding and provides medical benefits that are minimal for the financially needy. To qualify for this plan, you have to possess no more than a set dollar amount in property.

Medicare – A medical insurance program offered by the federal government to people who are age 65 or older, certain disabled people under the age of 65, and anyone with permanent kidney failure.

▶ **Part A** of this coverage is hospital insurance and **Part B** is medical insurance. **Part B** now comes with a monthly premium.

Medical Power of Attorney – Also known as health care power of attorney, this is the designation of a person who makes medical decisions for you when you cannot do it for yourself.

Minor Trust – A way to give gifts to a minor that avoids the gift tax and keeps the property safe until the minor becomes an adult and can take ownership of the trust.

Marital Trust – A trust for the surviving legal spouse of the deceased.

Mutual Will – A plan for your estate that is prepared in conjunction with another person.

N

Net Worth – A person's true financial value: Assets – Liabilities = Net Worth.

Non-charitable Trust – A trust that has a person or institution that is not a charity as the beneficiary.

Non-statutory Living Will – A legal document in which you spell out the decisions you have made about your medical care while you are still alive that does not comply with the laws of your state. A statutory document will likely provide more protection for the physicians and nurses carrying out your wishes.

Nuncupative Will – Also called an oral will, this is a spoken will. Some states, such as New York, only allow this kind of will if someone is literally on their deathbed, and it only covers personal property of little or no value. Again, you need to check with your state on the laws regarding this kind of will.

O

Opening Clauses – Lay out the basic information about who you are and set the stage for the clauses that follow. The *introductory clause* identifies you as the person who is making the will, the *family statement clause* introduces and identifies the family members who will be referred to later in the will, and the tax clause explains how the taxes on your estate will be paid.

Outright Charitable Gift – This is property you give to a charity and get nothing in return for; the gift can be cash or any other type of property.

Ownership – The individual(s) who hold the legal title to a piece of property; the ability to retain, sell, or give away this property depends on the number of people who hold that title, their relationship, and any legal agreements/contracts connected to the property.

▶ **Sole Ownership** – A single person holds the title to the property.

▶ **Joint Ownership** – When any two people hold an equal share of the title to a piece of property; the most common form is spousal, or when a legally married couple has both names on a title to a piece of property.

▶ **Community Property** – A state law that views a wife and husband as equal partners and assumes a 50/50 split of ownership. Indiana is not a community property state.

▶ **Separate Property** – Things owned by one spouse that are not part of the couple's community property.

▶ **Joint Tenancy** – A group of people hold an equal and undivided title to a piece of property.

P

Payable on Death (POD) – An account, like a savings account, that has a specific stipulation that the death of the original owner automatically transfers the ownership to a named beneficiary.

Pension Benefit Guarantee Corporation (PBGC) – A federal agency that can insure and therefore protect some or all of your pension, if your plan qualifies for the coverage and your company purchases the insurance.

Pension Plan – A program that is set up by an employer, including government agencies, to pay employees benefits upon retirement. Each employee has an individual account, and the employer makes a contribution to each employee's account based on the terms of the plan. There are two common types of pension plans.

▶ **Defined Benefit Plan** – A plan in which the employee will receive a specified amount of money upon retirement; the amount of the disbursement made is based on the number of years of employment.

▶ **Defined Contribution Plan** – A pension plan that sets a specific amount an employee will put into the plan (a percentage of income) and makes payments only for the amount of money contributed to the plan.

Phishing – The act of fraudulently representing an e-mail, Web site pop-up window, or other electronic communication as being from a bank, some other financial institution, or a legitimate business that requests the verification of personal information. These communications also request "missing" information and updates to intentionally incorrect data.

Pourover Will – This will place some property into a trust that was established while you were still alive.

Probate Court – The state-level court system that is specifically set up to handle all matters related to the distribution of a deceased person's estate; this is where a will is filed and unanswered questions about the disbursement of an estate are settled by a judge.

Profit Sharing Plan – Employees receive a portion of the profits earned by the company; the plan determines the amount that will be contributed to each employee's account.

Property – Also referred to as personal property, this comprises your possessions. This category is further divided into:

▶ **Real Property** – Any kind of real estate, such as a house, a condo, or a vacant lot.

▶ **Tangible Personal Property** – The things you can touch, such as a signed baseball, jewelry, or linen bed sheets.

▶ **Intangible Personal Property** – Checking accounts, savings accounts, money market funds, mutual funds, stocks, bonds, or retirement accounts, such as a pension, an IRA, a Roth IRA, or a Keogh plan.

Property Guardian – Also known as a property manager, this is a legal adult who takes responsibility for the oversight of property inherited by a minor/child. Children under the age of 18 can inherit property, but they can only be allowed to legally own that property with adult supervision; an adult must have the responsibility of managing it.

Property Interest – This refers to the connection a person has to a specific item, piece of land, or other items.

▶ **Legal Interest** – This is property that a person can legally transfer or manage, but it is not owned by the individual. Someone who is responsible for the maintenance and oversight of the use of a piece of property but who does not legally own it is called a trustee.

▶ **Beneficial Interest** – You receive a benefit from the property.

Protective Trusts – These are designed with conditions to protect the beneficiary's property.

Provisions – Clauses that explain how you want your wishes carried out.

Q

QTIP – A Qualified Terminable Interest Property trust is a marital deduction trust, but instead of your spouse deciding who gets the property after your death, the grantor makes that decision.

Qualified Pension Plan – A plan in which the amount of money that

the employer puts into an employee's account is not taxed as income during the fiscal year the contribution is made.

R

Renter's Insurance – The exchange of premiums for a guaranteed payment to cover the loss of personal property housed in rental property that is used as a primary residence.

Revocable – A trust that can be changed.

S

Simple Will – A legal document that identifies who you are, your beneficiaries, your executor, the directions you leave for the care of people for whom you are responsible, and the distribution of your assets.

Skimming – The act of using a special high-tech storage device to electronically "grab" account numbers and other information from a store computer register when a credit card transaction/purchase is processing.

Social Security Disability Benefit – Monthly payment made by the federal government to qualified recipients who can no longer work. Payments are made until the age of 65; at that point, you begin to receive the social security retirement benefits.

Social Security Retirement Benefit – Monthly payment made by the federal government to qualified recipients who reach retirement age. Payments are based on contributions made during the individual's employment period.

Social Security Supplemental Security Income (SSI) – The federal government makes a monthly payment to qualified individuals. This benefit is for people who have little (if any) property or are blind or disabled in some other way.

Special Needs Trust – A support trust for a disabled person under the age of 65. This trust makes payments on the beneficiaries' behalf, as required by the state as reimbursement. After the beneficiary dies, the property in the trust is paid to other beneficiaries. This trust is designed to protect your property from seizure by the government or a creditor seeking reimbursement.

Special Provisions – Encompasses all clauses that create specific requirements that are unique to the beneficiary or the assets. For example, a beneficiary of a trust might be required to be 21 or graduate college before he or she can take ownership of that trust.

Spendthrift Trust – A trust that is set up for someone who will not be able to handle his or her own affairs or who is mentally incompetent or might have financial problems and needs protection from creditors. The beneficiary does not own the property in the trust, just the payments that are made from the trust.

Spiritual Adviser – A minister, priest, monk, or some other cleric or individual trained in a specific faith tradition who offers guidance, support, and information related to his or her belief system.

Split-interest Trust – More than one individual benefits from the trust. One person or charity would have an interest in the trust for a specific period of time, and then another person or charity receives the property that remains.

State Estate Tax – A tax levied by the state on property left in an estate after a person dies, similar to the estate tax by the federal government, but the state tax is an additional tax burden. Not all states have an estate tax, but New York currently does.

State Gift Tax – A tax by individual states according to terms they set that is levied against any property you give to another person or institution during a fiscal year; it can be in cash or the transfer of property such as real estate or jewelry. Many of these are tied in some way to the federal estate tax.

State Income Tax – A tax on income earned during a fiscal year that is for residents of that state. Income earned in another state might be taxable in your state of residence, and any inheritance you receive that counts as income and is entered on your federal tax form can also be taxed.

Statutory Living Will – A legal document in which you spell out the decisions you have made about your medical care while you are still alive that complies with the statutes or laws of your state. A statutory document will likely provide more protection than a nonstatutory living will for the physicians and nurses carrying out your wishes.

Stock Bailout – The transfer of stock ownership from your name to that of a charity; the fair market value of the stock at the time of the transfer is the gift amount.

Stock Bonus Plan – A retirement plan established by an employer to give shares of the company's stock to employees. When the employee receives the shares, he must pay taxes based on the value of the stock.

▶ **Employee Stock Ownership Plan (ESOP)** – A retirement type of stock bonus plan. The employer contributes shares of its stock to a qualified trust, and the employee only pays taxes based on distributions he or she receives.

Successor Trustee – Someone who will step in if the primary trustee is unable to serve or cannot continue to manage your trust. This person will have the same legal obligations for managing the trust as the original trustee, should the successor assume the management responsibilities.

Supplemental Needs Trust – A support trust for a handicapped, elderly, or disabled person in need of support is assisted by this trust in such a way that it does not reduce or jeopardize the eligibility of that person to receive public or private benefits. This trust is designed to protect your property from seizure by the government or a creditor seeking reimbursement.

Support Trust – Requires a trustee to pay only the income and property necessary to cover the cost of education or assistance such as health care or nursing home fees of the beneficiaries.

Survival Clause – This leaves everything in your estate to one named person. Married people frequently do this to ensure that everything goes to the surviving spouse.

Survivor Benefit – A portion of the deceased employee's pension paid to the surviving spouse. The amount, regularly a percentage, is set by the terms of the pension plan rules.

T

Tax-Deferred – The taxes on money put into an investment account are paid when it is received by the employee in the form of a distribution, not at the time the money goes into the account.

Term Insurance – A life insurance policy that carries an annual premium and pays a specified death benefit to the beneficiary but does not have a cash value, so you cannot borrow money from it. The only payment made is to the beneficiary. The death benefit is not paid if premium payments are stopped.

▶ **Annual Renewable** – A term life policy that has an annual premium and can be renewed from year to year; be sure you understand the renewal rights before signing.

▶ **Decreasing** – A term life policy in which premiums remain the same but the benefit decreases over time. For example, if you purchase this kind of insurance (also called mortgage or credit term insurance) to pay off your debts after you die, the mortgage you want to insure might be $250,000 at the time you purchase the insurance, but the mortgage value when you die might be $150,000. The policy then pays $150,000. This kind of insurance is recommended only for those who cannot get any other kind of insurance.

▶ **Level** – A term life policy with coverage that is guaranteed for a specific period of time, or term, such as five, ten, or 20 years at a specific premium. The premium will remain for the five-year period, but at year six, it will go up and remain at that rate through the tenth year, continuing after that.

▶ **Group** – Employers frequently purchase a term life policy for each employee as an added benefit. Employees get an excellent low rate, and there is no income tax on the premiums for the first $50,000 of coverage.

Testamentary Trust – A fund created by the terms of your will after your death.

Testamentary Trust Will – This will moves your assets into one or more trusts after your death.

Testator – A person who writes a will.

Totten Trust – This is a bank account that, upon your death, immediately passes to the named beneficiary.

Trust – A legal arrangement that involves the transfer of property from the original owner to a person or a company for the purpose of holding and maintaining the property for the benefit of a specific individual, group of people, or institution(s).

Trustee – The person or company that will oversee or manage a financial resources account, such as a trust or custodian account, once it is established. This person or group will make sure the property in the trust is safe and in good order until it is turned over to the beneficiary.

Trust Agreement – The legal document that spells out the terms of a trust, including the people and conditions and the rules that must be followed; some are state or federal laws, and others are specific conditions.

Trustor – The person who sets up the trust. Other names commonly used are creator, donor, settlor, or grantor.

Trust Principal – The name given to property that is placed into a trust and is managed by a trust agreement.

U

Umbrella Liability Insurance – The exchange of premiums for a guaranteed payment to cover a host of situations that would put personal property at risk, such as personal liability or negligence.

V

Vested – To meet the predetermined requirements contained within a pension plan based on the number of years you have worked for the employer. Before an employee can receive any distributions or take full ownership of a pension plan, the employee has to be fully vested.

W

Waiver – A written statement declining the right to receive benefits signed by a spouse. This waiver must be signed to legally sever the right to claim any benefits — an alternative agreement, such as signing a prenuptial agreement, will not be enough.

Whole Life Insurance – Sometimes called "cash value" life insurance, this is a form of life insurance for which the insured person pays a monthly or annual premium to a company that will, upon the owner's death, pay a pre-

determined, fixed amount of money to the beneficiaries. A portion of the fixed (meaning it will never go up or down) premium is invested, another portion is placed into an account, like a savings account, and that cash value is accessible to the policy owner. It can be borrowed against as a loan, or the cash can be taken as the proceeds of the policy instead of the death benefit payout.

- ▶ **Universal Life** – A kind of whole life policy that guarantees a minimum return, but the value of the policy can go up or down. If the policy makes more money, the return might be high enough to cover your premium payments.

- ▶ **Joint First-to-Die or Second-to-Die** – Just as it sounds, this is a policy held by two people, and the beneficiary is paid after the first or second person dies, as designated in the policy.

Will – A legal document in which you identify which people or institutions will receive money and property from your estate after your death; it also serves to appoint guardianship of children or adults who are your legal responsibility and designates an executor to manage your estate after you die.

Will Substitute – An agreement, contract, or other legal arrangement that will accomplish the same goals of a will — to protect and transfer property rights — but without the use of a will document.

BIBLIOGRAPHY

"Do I have to pay taxes on a life insurance death benefit?" **http://www. wwwebtax.com/income/life_insurance_proceeds.htm**. Accessed on July 8, 2010.

Family Court Forms, New York CourtHelp, New York State Unified Court System, **http://www.nycourts.gov/courthelp/forms.html**. Accessed June 25, 2010.

Glass v. Battista, 43 N.Y.2d 620 (1978) ("Where two people sign joint or mutual wills and one of them dies, the survivor is bound to the terms of the will and may not make a different testamentary disposition or inter vivos gift that would defeat the purpose of the joint will agreement.")

"Gift Tax." Internal Revenue Service. **http://www.irs.gov/businesses/ small/article/0,,id=164872,00.html**. Accessed on January 26, 2010.

Laws of New York (New York Code). **http://public.leginfo.state.ny.us/**. Accessed on July 5, 2010.

"Majority of American Adults Remain without Wills New Lawyers.com Survey Finds." Harris Interactive. **http://www.harrisinteractive.com/news/newsletters/clientnews/2007_Lawyers.pdf.** Accessed on January 26, 2010.

"Medicaid in New York State." **http://www.nyhealth.gov/health_care/medicaid/index.htm**. Accessed on July 7, 2010.

New York Civil Practice Law and Rules. **http://public.leginfo.state.ny.us.** Accessed on July 8, 2010.

New York Department of Taxation and Finance. **http://www.tax.state.ny.us**. Accessed on June 25, 2010.

"Proceeds From Taxes and Insurance." *Estate Planning*. HSBC – North America Military Financial Education Center. University of Maryland University College. **http://militaryfinance.umuc.edu/estate/estateplan_taxes.html**. Accessed on June 25, 2010.

U.S. Department of Labor. Bureau of Labor Statistics. **http://www.bls.gov**. Accessed on January 26, 2010.

BIOGRAPHY

Linda C. Ashar has practiced law for more than 25 years before the Ohio and federal bars. In addition to Atlantic Publishing Group's estate-planning series, she has authored *101 Ways to Score Higher on Your LSAT: What You Need to Know About the Law School Admission Test Explained Simply*, *The Complete Power of Attorney Guide for Consumers and Small Businesses: Everything You Need to Know Explained Simply*, poetry, and several magazine and journal articles, including a collection on **Suite101.com**.

Ashar and her lawyer-husband, Mike, operate Thornapple Farms in Vermilion, Ohio, where they breed Morgan horses, Connemara ponies, and Irish Kerry Bog ponies, a critically endangered breed. Ashar serves on several nonprofit boards and is co-founder of the American Kerry Bog Pony Society. Reach her at ashar@hbr.net or lashar@wickenslaw.com.

Empire State Building, New York City

INDEX

147, 193, 200, 220-221, 269, 272-274, 277-278, 280

P

Parchment, 64

Pension Plan, 72, 143, 145-147, 153, 220, 247, 274-276, 278, 280

Pourover Will, 275

Probate Court Judge, 54, 56

Property Guardian, 50, 275

Property Manager, 50, 275

Protective trust, 119, 121, 269

R

Residuary Clause, 101, 111, 270

S

Separate Property, 62, 274

Simple Will, 99, 104, 276

Sole Ownership, 62, 274

Spendthrift Trust, 122, 277

Statutory Living Will, 106, 278

Stock Bailout, 82, 278

Successor Trustee, 115, 278

Survival Clause, 100, 278

T

Terminal Condition, 198

Testamentary Trust Will, 104, 279

Totten Trust, 122, 279

Trust, 23, 27, 34, 50, 52-53, 55, 57, 61, 63, 66-68, 72-74, 76, 78, 86, 98, 104-105, 109, 113-126, 128, 136, 147, 153, 163, 167-169, 172173-176, 178, 186, 193-194, 199-200, 202, 204-206, 211, 217, 223, 247-248, 261-264, 266-273, 275-280

U

Umbrella Liability Insurance, 135, 280

Universal Life, 137-138, 280

V

Values List, 21, 25

Video Will, 104

W

Well, 11, 15-16, 21, 26, 39, 42, 49, 53, 57-58, 78, 84, 90, 97, 106, 109-110, 133, 135, 146, 149, 163, 165, 173, 184, 192, 195, 198, 204, 214, 266

Whole Life, 137-138, 141, 280